THE LIFE OF KIT CARSON

HUNTER, TRAPPER, GUIDE, INDIAN AGENT AND COLONEL U.S.A.

By
Edward S. Ellis.

Copyright © 2016 Read Books Ltd.
This book is copyright and may not be
reproduced or copied in any way without
the express permission of the publisher in writing

British Library Cataloguing-in-Publication Data
A catalogue record for this book is available from
the British Library

CONTENTS

Edward S. Ellis 5
Introduction 9

CHAPTER I. 11
CHAPTER II. 17
CHAPTER III. 23
CHAPTER IV. 29
CHAPTER V. 35
CHAPTER VI. 41
CHAPTER VII. 47
CHAPTER VIII. 53
CHAPTER IX 58
CHAPTER X. 64
CHAPTER XI. 70
CHAPTER XII. 76
CHAPTER XIII. 81
CHAPTER XIV. 86
CHAPTER XV. 92
CHAPTER XVI. 97

CHAPTER XVII.	102
CHAPTER XVIII.	108
CHAPTER XIX.	114
CHAPTER XX	120
CHAPTER XXI.	126
CHAPTER XXII.	132
CHAPTER XXIII.	144
CHAPTER XXIV.	153
CHAPTER XXV.	160
CHAPTER XXVI.	166
CHAPTER XXVII.	171
CHAPTER XXVIII.	177
CHAPTER XXIX.	183
CHAPTER XXX.	188
CHAPTER XXXI.	194
CHAPTER XXXII.	200
CHAPTER XXXIII.	204
CHAPTER XXXIV.	210
CHAPTER XXXV.	215
CHAPTER XXXVI.	220
CHAPTER XXXVII.	225
CHAPTER XXXVIII.	231

Edward S. Ellis

Edward Sylvester Ellis was born on 11 April 1840 to the marksman and hunter, Sylvester Ellis, and his wife, Mary Ellis, in Geneva, Ashtabula County, Ohio. When Ellis was six, the family moved to New Jersey where Ellis attended school. This association with school and education lasted as Ellis worked as a teacher for a number of years, first at Red Bank, New Jersey, then later as a member of faculty at the state normal school in Trenton – where he had studied when he was younger. He then worked as a teacher at Raritan, New Jersey, then as a vice principal of a public school at Paterson, before becoming principal of one of the largest schools in Trenton. He followed this by becoming the superintendent of schools in the same city. He was a member of the Board of Education and in 1887 received his degree of Master of Arts from Princeton College. Ellis began writing during his time as a teacher, but continued working within the education system until the mid-1880s. After leaving education, he devoted his life to literature.

Ellis wrote throughout much of his life and had over 159 novels published in his name, as well as a number of other novels and articles that he published under a variety of pseudonyms. These pseudonyms included, among others: Captain Bruin Adams (under which he had 68 titles published), Emerson

Rodman (ten titles), Lieutenant Ned Hunter (five titles), and Seelin Robins (nineteen titles). Ellis had his first poems published in *Gleeson's Pictorial* in 1857. His novel, *Dick Flinton, or Life on the Border* appeared in the *New York Dispatch* as a serial in 1859, and reappeared later as *Kent the Ranger* in 1863 as a dime novel. During this time Ellis under contract to Beadle and Company for four novels a year.

The novel that brought Ellis to the public's attention was *Seth Jones, or the Captives of the Frontier* (1860) which galvanised the dime novel phenomenon. It was extensively advertised at the time and sold over 500,000 copies. 60,000 copies were sold within the first week of its release and it was rumoured to have been a favourite of Abraham Lincoln. Ellis was best known internationally for his *Deerfoot* novels which were read widely by young boys until the 1950s. They depict life at the beginning of the white settlement in America and the encounters and adventures of four travellers. Ellis's other titles included: *The Steam Man of the Prairies* (1868), *The Rival Hunters* (1875), and *Bill Biddon, Trapper* (1860). In the mid-1880s, Ellis moved away from children's fiction and began writing more serious biographies, histories and persuasive pieces. These included his novel *The Life of Colonel Davis Crockett* (1884) which told the story of the speech Davy Crockett gave in opposition to the awarding of money to a naval widow.

Ellis was married twice. He married Anna M. Deane on December 25 1862 and with her he had one son, Willmott Edward Ellis, and three daughters. Anna and Ellis divorced in 1887, and Ellis married Clara Spaulding-Brown on November 20 1960. The pair had met previously as she was a novelist and had also worked on the staff of *Golden Days* when Ellis was an associate editor from 1878-1879. He also edited *Public Opinion*, a Trenton daily, from 1874-1875 and was the editor of the *Boys Holiday*, later *The Holiday*, from 1890-1891. Ellis was a prolific writer until his death on a vacation trip in Cliff Island, Maine on June 20 1916.

INTRODUCTION

Christopher Carson, or as he was familiarly called, Kit Carson, was a man whose real worth was understood only by those with whom he was associated or who closely studied his character. He was more than hunter, trapper, guide, Indian agent and Colonel in the United States Army. He possessed in a marked degree those mental and moral qualities which would have made him prominent in whatever pursuit or profession he engaged.

His lot was cast on the extreme western frontier, where, when but a youth, he earned the respect of the tough and frequently lawless men with whom he came in contact. Integrity, bravery, loyalty to friends, marvelous quickness in making right decisions, in crisis of danger, consummate knowledge of woodcraft, a leadership as skilful as it was daring; all these were distinguishing traits in the composition of Carson and were the foundations of the broader fame which he acquired as the friend and invaluable counselor of Fremont, the Pathfinder, in his expeditions across the Rocky Mountains.

Father Kit, as he came to be known among the Indians, risked his life scores of times for those who needed, but had no special claim upon his services. The red men were quick to learn that he always spoke with a "single tongue," and that he was their unselfish friend. He went among his hostiles when no one of his race dare follow him; he averted more than one outbreak; he secured that which is impossible to secure—justice for the Indian—and his work from the time when a mere boy he left his native Kentucky, was always well done. His memory will forever remain fragrant with those who appreciate true manhood and an unswerving devotion to the good of those among whom he lived and died.

CHAPTER I.

KIT CARSON'S YOUTH—HIS VISIT TO NEW MEXICO—ACTS AS INTERPRETER AND INVARIOUS OTHER EMPLOYMENTS—JOINS A PARTY OF TRAPPERS AND ENGAGES IN A FIGHT WITH INDIANS—VISITS THE SACRAMENTO VALLEY.

"Kit Carson," the most famous hunter, scout and guide ever known in this country, was a native of Kentucky, the scene of the principal exploits of Daniel Boone, Simon Kenton, the Wetzel brothers and other heroic pioneers whose names are identified with the history of the settlement of the West.

Christopher Carson was born in Madison county, December 24, 1809, and, while he was still an infant, his father removed to Central Missouri, which at that day was known as Upper Louisiana. It was an immense wilderness, sparsely settled and abounding with wild animals and treacherous Indians. The father of Carson, like most of the early pioneers, divided his time between cultivating the land and hunting the game in the forests. His house was made strong and was pierced with loopholes, so as to serve him in his defence against the red men that were likely to attack him and his family at any hour of the day or night. In such a school was trained the wonderful scout, hunter and guide.

No advantages in the way of a common school education were within reach of the youth situated as was Kit Carson. It is to be believed, however, that under the tutelage of his father and mother, he picked up a fair knowledge of the rudimentary branches, for his attainments in that respect were above the majority of those with whom he was associated in after life.

While a mere stripling, Kit became known as one of the most skilful rifle shots in that section of Missouri which produced some of the finest marksmen in the world. It was inevitable that he should form a passion for the woods, in which, like the great Boone, he would have been happy to wander for days and weeks at a time.

When fifteen years old, he was apprenticed to a saddler, where he stayed two years. At the end of that time, however, the confinement had become so irksome that he could stand it no longer. He left the shop and joined a company of traders, preparing to start for Santa Fe, the capital of New Mexico, one of the most interesting towns in the southwest. The majority of its population are of Spanish and Mexican origin and speak Spanish. It is the centre of supplies for the surrounding country, and is often a scene of great activity. It stands on a plateau, more than a mile above the sea level, with another snow capped mountain rising a mile higher. The climate is delightful and the supply of water from the springs and mountains is of the finest quality.

Santa Fe, when first visited by the Spaniards in 1542, was a populous Indian pueblo. It has been the capital of New Mexico for nearly two hundred and fifty years. The houses of the ancient town are made of adobe, one story high, and the streets

The Mexicans have never been particularly friendly toward their neighbors north of the Rio Grande, and at that time a very strict law was in force which forbade the issuance of any license to American citizens to trap within Mexican territory. The company which mounted their horses and rode out of Taos gave the authorities to understand that their errand was simply to chastise the red men, whereas their real purpose was to engage in trapping. With a view of misleading the officers, they took a roundabout route which delayed their arrival in the section. Nevertheless, the hunters were desirous of punishing the Indians who had taken such liberties with the small party that preceded them. On one of the tributaries of the Gila, the trappers came upon the identical band whom they attacked with such fierceness that more than a dozen were killed and the rest put to flight. The fight was a desperate one, but young as Carson was, he acquitted himself in a manner which won the warmest praise of those with him. He was unquestionably daring, skilful and sagacious, and was certain, if his life was spared, to become one of the most valuable members of the party.

Having driven the savages away, the Americans began or rather resumed their regular business of trapping. The beavers were so abundant that they met with great success. When the rodents seemed to diminish in number, the hunters shifted their quarters, pursuing their profession along the numerous streams until it was decided to divide into two parties, one of which returned to New Mexico, while the other pushed on toward the Sacramento Valley in California. Carson accompanied the latter, entering the region at that early day when no white man dreamed of the vast wealth of gold and precious metals which so crowded her soil and river beds that the wonder is the gleaming particles had not been detected many years before; but, as the reader knows, they lay quietly at rest until that eventful day in 1848, when the secret was revealed by Captain Sutter's raceway and the frantic multitudes flocked thither from the four quarters of the earth.

CHAPTER II.

CALIFORNIA—SUFFERINGS OF THE HUNTERS—THE MISSION OF SAN GABRIEL—THE HUDSON BAY TRAPPERS—CHARACTERISTICS OF CARSON—HE LEADS THE PARTY WHICH CAPTURES AN INDIAN VILLAGE AND SECURES SOME CRIMINALS.

California, one of the most magnificent regions of the earth, with its amazing mineral wealth, its rich soil and "glorious climate," has its belts of sterility and desolation, where the bones of many a traveller and animal lie bleaching in the sun, just as they fell years ago, when the wretched victim sank down and perished for want of food and water.

The hunting party to which Carson was attached numbered eighteen, and they entered one of those forbidding wastes, where they suffered intensely. All their skill in the use of the rifle was of no avail, when there was no game to shoot and it was not long before they were forced to live on horse flesh to escape starvation. This, however, was not so trying as might be supposed, provided it did not last until the entire party were dismounted.

Fortunately, in their straits, they encountered a party of Mohave Indians, who sold them enough food to remove all danger. These Indians form a part of the Yuma nation of the Pima family, and now make their home on the Mohave and Colorado rivers in Arizona. They are tall, well formed, warlike and industrious cultivators of the soil. Had they chosen to attack the hunters, it would have gone ill with the whites, but the latter showed commendable prudence which might have served as a model to the hundreds who came after them, when they gained the good will of the red men.

Extricating themselves from the dangerous stretch of country, the trappers turned westward until they reached the mission of San Gabriel, one of those extensive establishments formed by the Roman Catholic clergy a hundred years ago. There were over a score, San Diego being the oldest. Each mission had its priests, a few Spanish or Mexican soldiers, and scores, hundreds and sometimes thousands of Indian converts who received a scant support and some religious instruction.

The Mission of San Gabriel was by no means the largest in California, and yet at the time of Carson's visit it owned 70,000 head of cattle, 200 horses, 3,000 mares, hundreds of mules, oxen and sheep, while the vineyards produced 600 barrels of wine every year.

Those old sovereigns of the soil dispensed hospitality without stint to all who knocked at their gates. When the trappers caught sight of the Mission, as they rode out from the wilderness, they knew what awaited them in the way of entertainment. They were treated right royally, but remained only one day.

Not far away they reached another Mission of less extent than the former, but, without halt, they pressed steadily forward toward the Sacramento River. The character of the section changed altogether. It was exceedingly fertile and game was so abundant that they feasted to their heart's content. When fully rested, they proceeded to the San Joaquin river down which they began trapping.

While thus employed, they were surprised to discover signs of another trapping party near them. They wondered where they came from and it did not take them long to learn that their neighbors were a company of trappers belonging to the Hudson Bay Company—that enormous corporation, founded two centuries before, whose agents and employees tramp over British America, far to the northward of the frozen circle, and until a recent date hunted through Oregon.

The two parties were rivals in business, but they showed excellent sense by meeting on good terms and treating each other as friends. They trapped near each other until they came to the Sacramento once more, when they parted company. The Hudson Bay trappers started for the Columbia River, while the one to which Carson was attached went into camp where they were for the rest of the summer. With the approach of warm weather the trapping season ended and they devoted themselves to hunting and making ready for cold weather.

It will be borne in mind that Kit Carson was still a youth, not having reached his majority. He was of short, compact stature, no more than five feet, six inches tall, with light brown hair, gray eyes, large head, high forehead, broad shoulders, full chest, strong and possessing remarkable activity. Even at that early age, he had impressed the veteran hunters and trappers around him as one possessing such remarkable abilities, that, if his life was spared, he was certain to become a man of mark. If we should attempt to specify the particular excellencies in which he surpassed those around him, it would be said that while Carson was one of the most fearless men who lived, yet he possessed splendid judgment. He seemed to know instinctively what could be accomplished by himself and friends in positions of extreme peril, and he saw on the moment precisely how to do that which often was impossible to others.

His knowledge of woodcraft and the peculiarities of the savage tribes around him was as perfect as it could be. He was a matchless hunter, and no man could handle a rifle with greater skill. The wilderness, the mountains, the Indians, the wild animals—these constituted the sphere in which nature intended Kit Carson should move and serve his fellow men as no one before or after him has done.

Added to these extraordinary qualifications, was the crowning one of all—modesty. Alas, how often transcendent merit is made repelling by overweening conceit. Kit Carson would have given his life before he would have travelled through the eastern cities, with his long hair dangling about his shoulders, his clothing bristling with pistols and knives, while he strutted on the mimic stage as a representative of the untamed civilization of the great west.

Carson was a superior hunter when a boy in Missouri, and the experience gained among the experienced hunters and trappers, soon caused him to become noted by those who had fought red men, trapped beaver and shot grizzly bears before he was born. And yet it could not have been that alone: it must have been his superior mental capacity which caused those heroes of a hundred perils to turn instinctively to him for counsel and guidance in situations of extreme peril. Among them all was no one with such masterful resources in that respect as he.

While the trappers were encamped at this place, a messenger

visited them from the Mission of San Rafael, with a request that they would help chastise a party of Indians, who, after committing some outrages at the Mission, had fled to an Indian village. When a demand was made for the surrender of the refugees, the villagers not only refused to give them up, but attacked the party and drove them off. Appreciating the importance of upholding their authority, the priests sent to the trappers for assistance in bringing the guilty ones and their friends to terms.

As soon as the request was made known, Carson and eleven of his companions volunteered to help their visitors. Thus reinforced, the company from the Mission set out again for the Indian village.

Nothing can attest more strongly the skill and bravery of Kit Carson, than the fact that he was at once selected to lead the party on its dangerous errand. While he was as modest as a woman and with a voice as gentle and persuasive, he could not be ignorant of his own capacities, and he assumed charge without any pretense of unfitness.

It is easy to understand the great care required in this expedition, for the warriors in the village, having beaten off their assailants, naturally looked for their return with reinforcements, and, in order to insure success, it was necessary that the attack should be a surprise.

Having brought his men quite close to the village unperceived, Kit gave the signal and the whole company swept through the place like a cyclone. There were a few minutes of terrific fighting, during which a score of warriors were killed, and then the entire village was captured. Carson as the leader of the assailants, demanded the surrender of the offenders against the Mission. Not daring to disobey such a summons, they were delivered up to the authorities, and Carson, seeing nothing more to do for his friends, returned with his companions to camp and resumed hunting and their preparations for cold weather.

CHAPTER III.

THE TRAPPER'S LIFE—INDIAN HORSE THIEVES—CARSON'S SKILFUL PURSUIT AND SURPRISE OF THE SAVAGES—ARRIVAL AT LOS ANGELES—TROUBLE WITH THE AUTHORITIES—A SINGULAR ESCAPE.

The trappers being in the heart of the Indian country, with hostile on every hand, were cautious in all their movements. When one of the grizzled hunters in the depths of the wilderness fired his gun at some deer, antelope or bear, he hastily reloaded his rifle, listening meanwhile for sounds of the stealthy footprints of his enemy. He knew not when the treacherous shot would be sent from behind the rock or clump of bushes, but he had learned long before, that, when he penetrated the western wilds and followed the calling of trapper, he took his life in his hands and he was ready to "go under," whenever the fate so decreed.

The most flagrant crime on the frontier is horse stealing. He who shoots one of his fellow men has a chance of escaping punishment almost as good as that afforded in civilized communities, but if he steals a horse and is caught, his case is hopeless. It may be said that the value of the animal to the hunter or trapper is beyond all calculation, and, inasmuch as the red man is equally appreciative, Carson always warned his friends to be on the watch against the dusky thieves. Sentinels were on guard while others slept, but the very calamity against which they thus sought to protect themselves overtook them.

One dark night a number of Indians stole by the sentinels and before their presence was discovered, drove off the major part of the horses. In the morning, when the alarming truth became known, the employer of the trappers asked Carson to take twelve of the men and do his utmost to recover those that were stolen. Carson assented at once, and, in his quiet, self possessed fashion, collected his comrades who were speedily in the saddle and galloping along the trail of the thieves.

It may strike the reader that an offhand statement like the foregoing relates to a proceeding of no special difficulty or peril. A party of brave white men were pursuing a company of Indian horse thieves and the chances of escape and capture were about equal. Thus the matter presents itself to the ordinary spectator, whereas the truth was far different.

In the first place, the savages, being as well mounted as their pursuers, were sure to maintain a swift pace, so long as they believed any danger threatened. They would keep a keen watch of the back trail and would be quick to detect the approach of enemies. If pressed hard, they would act as the Apaches and Comanches do, when they find the United States troops at their heels—break up in so many small parties that it is impossible to follow them.

First of all, therefore, Carson had two achievements before him—and the accomplishment of either seemed to render the other impossible: he must travel at a faster rate than the thieves, and, at the same time keep them in ignorance of his pursuit. It is on such occasions that a man's woodcraft and knowledge of the country serve him so well. Many a time, during the career of Kit Carson, did he outwit the red men and white criminals, not by galloping along with his eye upon their footprints, but by reasoning out with unerring skill, the destination or refuge which the criminals had in mind. Having settled that all important question, he aimed at the same point and frequently reached it first. Thus it came about that often the fugitive, while hurrying along and glancing furtively behind him, suddenly found himself face to face with his pursuer, whose acquaintance with the country enabled him to find the shorter route.

It took Carson only a few minutes to satisfy himself that the criminals were heading for the Sierra Nevada Mountains, but, inasmuch as they were following a direct course, he could only take their trail. Where there were so many animals in flight, it was impossible to hide their tracks and the thieves made no attempt to do so. They struck the horses into a sweeping gallop, which with a few interruptions they maintained until they were a hundred miles from the camp of the white men and among the fastnesses of the Sierras.

Then it was the red men made a careful survey of the trail behind them. The black penetrating eyes scanned the country with a piercing keenness which it would seem shut out all possibility of concealment. Nowhere could they detect the faint smoke climbing toward the sky from among the trees nor could they gain sight of the line of horsemen winding around the rocks in the distance. Nothing resembling a human being was visible. Surely they were warranted in believing themselves perfectly secure.

Such being their conclusion, they prepared for a great feast.

Six of the stolen horses were killed and the red men became as ardent hipophagi as was the club of advanced Parisians a short time ago. The roasted meat tasted as fine to them as though it was the choicest slices from the bison or deer, and they ate and frolicked like so many children let loose for a holiday.

But in the midst of their feast was heard a series of frightful yells and whoops. The appalled Indians had scarcely time to turn their eyes when a dozen horsemen, that seemed to have risen from the very ground, thundered down upon them. Carson and his men had overtaken the thieves and they now swept down upon them with resistless fury. The fight was as short as it was fierce. The red men fell on the right and left, and those who escaped the wrath of the trappers, scattered and ran as if a hundred bomb shells were exploding around them. Every horse stolen (except the six killed for the feast) were recovered and Carson took them back to camp without the loss of a man.

The hunters stayed until early autumn, when their employer decided to go to New Mexico. The journey led for a great portion of the way through a country over which they had travelled, and which therefore was familiar to them. After halting a brief while at the Mission of San Fernando, they arrived at Los Angeles, which like the rest of the country as the reader knows, belonged to Mexico. As it was apparent that the horsemen were hunters and trappers, the authorities demanded their written license to pursue their calling in Mexican territory. Such was the law and the officials were warranted in making the demand, but it need not be said that the party were compelled to admit they had nothing of the kind in their possession.

The authorities thereupon determined to arrest the hunters, but knowing their desperate nature, hesitated as to the safe means of doing so. They finally hit upon a rather ingenious, though unfair means of disarming the white men: they began giving them "fire water" to drink, refusing to accept pay therefor. Those who lead lives of hardship and peril are generally fond of such indulgence, and, though the trappers could not fail to understand the purpose of the Mexicans, and though they knew the disastrous consequences of giving away to temptation, they yielded and took in their mouths the enemy which stole away their brains.

The employer became alarmed and saw that something must be done at once or everything would be lost. Carson had been too wise to fall into the snare, and he turned to him.

"Take three of the soberest men," said he, "and the loose animals and camp equipage and push out of the place. I will join you as soon as I can, but you mustn't linger for me. If I fail to join you, hasten to New Mexico and make known that I and the rest of my men have been massacred."

These instructions were definite and they showed the gravity of the situation. Carson did as directed, while the employer gave his attention to the rest of the men. It was high time that he did so, for they were fast succumbing to their appetites. Despite the indignant protests and efforts of the employer they would have undoubtedly fallen victims but for an unlooked for occurrence.

One of the trappers who was so much under the influence of liquor as to become reckless, fired upon and slightly wounded a native of the place. The act threw the Mexicans into a panic of terror, and they fled from the presence of the dreaded Americans who seemed eager for any sanguinary deed.

The employer was wise enough to take advantage of the occurrence and he succeeded, after much labor, in getting his half intoxicated men together and out of the place. The horses were forced to their utmost and the same night they overtook Carson and his anxious companions. All danger from that source was ended.

CHAPTER IV.

AN ALARMING VISIT—CARSON'S RESOURCES—ON THE COLORADO AND GILA—CAPTURING A HERD OF HORSES AND MULES—THE RAIDERS—TURNING THE TABLES—CACHING THEIR PELTRIES—RETURN TO SANTA FE—CARSON GOES UPON A SECOND TRAPPING EXPEDITION—HUNTING WITH AN OLD MOUNTAINEER—A VISIT FROM CROW INDIANS.

A week or more later, the trappers again reached the Colorado River. They had traveled at a leisurely pace and once more they went into camp, where they were familiar with the country. Men leading such lives as they, were accustomed to all kinds of surprises, but it may be doubted whether the trappers were more amazed in all their existence than when five hundred Indian warriors made their appearance and with signs of friendship overran the camp before they could be prevented or checked.

The hunters did not know what to make of the proceeding, and looked to Carson for advice. He had already discovered that the situation was one of the gravest danger. Despite the professions of friendship, Kit saw that each warrior had his weapons under his dress, where he hoped they were not noticed by the whites. Still worse, most of the hunters were absent visiting their traps, only Kit and a few of his companions being in camp. The occasion was where it was necessary to decide at once what to do and then to do it without flinching.

Among the red men was one who spoke Spanish and to him Carson addressed himself:

"You must leave the camp at once; if you don't do so without a minute's delay, we shall attack you and each of us is sure to kill one warrior if not more."

These brave words accompanied by such determination of manner were in such contrast to the usual course of the cowardly Mexicans that the Indians were taken all aback. They could not suspect the earnestness of the short, sturdy framed leader, nor could they doubt that though the Indians would be sure to overwhelm the little band, yet they would have to pay dearly for the privilege. It took them but a few minutes to conclude the price was altogether too high and they drew off without making a hostile demonstration against the brave Carson and his men.

The trappers worked their way down the Colorado until they arrived at tidewater, when they moved to the Gila, along which they trapped until they reached the mouth of the San Pedro. They were in sore need of horses with which to transport their furs and peltries, that had become numerous and bulky. While in this neighborhood, they discovered a large herd of horses and mules in the possession of a few Indians. According to the morality of the border this property was legitimate prey, but in point of fact when the trappers determined to take the animals from the aborigines, they became thieves and robbers. However, it is not to be hoped that a single member of the company felt the slightest twinge of conscience when he rode at full speed, yelling to the highest bent, and helped scatter the terrified red men to the winds. The entire herd fell into the hands of the whites, and, congratulating themselves on their good fortune, they kindled a huge fire and encamped for the night.

Most of the men had lain down with the intention of sleeping until morning, and Kit sat looking in the fire, when his trained ear caught a peculiar sound. At first, it seemed to be the faint roll of distant thunder, but he knew it was not. He listened carefully and was able to tell the direction whence came the singular noise, but remained uncertain as to its cause. Then, as he had done many a time, he leaned over and pressed his ear to the solid earth. Immediately the rumbling became more distinct and he recognized what it meant: it was the tramp of numerous hoofs galloping forward.

Carson and several of his men stole noiselessly out to reconnaissance and found a half dozen warriors hurrying along a drove of more than a hundred horses. They had been on a raid among the Mexican settlements in Sonora and were now returning home with their plunder.

The temptation was one which Carson and his companions could not resist. They sent a volley from their rifles among the thieves, which threw them into such a panic that they dashed off at full speed without giving the least thought to their valuable property. The latter as a matter of course was taken charge of by the trappers, who were glad of the opportunity to chastise the cowardly marauders.

Under the circumstances, however, the animals were of little value to the hunters, who had all they needed. It was beyond their power to return them to their owners, but the best were selected, several of the plumpest killed and cured, and the rest turned loose to go whither they chose.

The trappers continued up the Gila until near the copper mines of New Mexico, where they found a party of white men trading with the Indians. The peltries were cached and placed in charge of their friends, while Carson and his companions continued on until they reached Santa Fe. There their employer bought a license to trade with the Indians who lived near the copper mines. Then they went back and procuring their furs, returned once more to Santa Fe, where they were sold for more than twenty thousand dollars. This being equitably divided among the hunters, furnished each a goodly sum. Like so many sailors just ashore from a long voyage, most of the trappers went on a prolonged carousal, which caused their money to melt like snow in the sun. When their pockets were empty, they had aching heads, weak frames and only the memory of their feverish pleasures.

Kit Carson did not go through this trial unscathed. He drank and spreed with the rest, but he awoke to the folly and madness of his course sooner than they and the sad lesson learned at the time lasted him through life. The baneful habit was not fastened upon him, and he not only acquired the mastery over self, but was able more than once to save others from falling into the whirlpool which has swept unnumbered multitudes to wretchedness and death.

Carson found little in the way of congenial employment until the fall of the year, when he joined a second trapping expedition. The first had won him such a reputation for sagacity, daring and skill, that his services were always in demand, and those who were forming such enterprises sought him out among the very first.

The new party was in charge of an experienced mountaineer, who told Kit his intention was to trap along the principal streams of the Rocky Mountains. He was well acquainted with the region and was confident that the expedition would not only be enjoyable and thrilling in the highest degree, but would prove profitable to all.

The party travelled northward until they reached the Platte River where the business began. They moved from stream to stream, as necessity demanded, shooting such game as they needed, exchanging shots with the watchful red men, who killed four of the trappers while hunting bison, and steadily adding to their stock of furs until the close of the season in the spring of 1831. Learning that an old mountaineer, named Captain Gaunt, had spent the winter at Laramie River and was then at New Park, Kit Carson and four of his friends set out to join him. It was a long and perilous journey, but they made it in safety and the Captain gave them glad welcome. They hunted together for many months following until the Captain went to Taos to sell his peltries. On his return, operations were resumed until the weather became so cold they were forced into winter quarters.

The winter proved very severe. The snow was so deep that only by cutting down numerous cottonwoods and using the bark and twigs for fodder were the animals saved from starvation. Fortunately, they had laid in a good stock of bison meat so that the trappers themselves underwent no suffering for food. In fact, they found little to do except to pass the time in idleness. With abundant food, plenty of tobacco and the means of engaging in certain games, they whiled away the long winter days and evenings until the signs of spring appeared.

But while the winds were moaning around their hut, in which they made their home, and the snow rattled like fine sand against the logs, they were taught again that no weather is severe enough to keep the wily red man within his wigwam. A party of Crow Indians discovered the camp of the trappers and one tempestuous night made them a stealthy visit. They departed during the darkness, and, when they went away, took with them nine of the very best horses of the hunters—a loss too serious to be borne without using every recourse to prevent it.

CHAPTER V.

KIT CARSON'S DECISION—A HOT PURSUIT AN AND UNEXPECTED DISCOVERY—WEARY WAITING—A SNOW BALLING PARTY—A DARING ATTACK—BRILLIANT EXPLOIT.

Instinctively every one turned to Carson to learn what he had to advise and yet each was certain what he would say.

"It'll never do, boys, to let them steal our horses in that style," he remarked in his quiet fashion, compressing his lips and shaking his head, while his eyes flashed with a dangerous light.

All knew what his words and manner meant, and in a twinkling the thirteen men were in their saddles, and, with their gallant leader at their head, galloped forth off in pursuit.

It would be supposed where the ground was covered with snow to such a depth, that it was the easiest matter imaginable to follow the trail, and yet Kit and his companions found it one of the most difficult tasks they had ever undertaken. Hundreds of bison had repeatedly crossed the tracks since they were made and less experienced eyes than those of the trappers would have given over the search in despair.

But no one thought of turning back, and the pursuit was

pushed unflaggingly for fully forty miles. Not the first glimpse had been obtained of the Indians, and the horses that had been pushed so hard finally gave out. They were in poor condition, and, when the company came to a halt, showed such exhaustion that it was evident they could not be forced much further. It was decided, therefore, to go into camp. Accordingly, they turned the heads of their panting animals toward a piece of woods a short distance away.

Before the shelter was reached, the trappers were astonished to observe a column of smoke rising above the trees. They looked in each others' faces with a smile of gratification: inasmuch as the trail led into the grove and it was evident a camp fire was burning there, it followed that they were close to the thieves whom they had followed such a long distance.

The discovery infused new warmth into the blood of the hunters, who were fairly atremble with eagerness to attack the unsuspecting Indians.

But all were too experienced in the ways of the wilderness to allow their impatience to betray them into any indiscretion. They deemed it necessary their assault should be a surprise and they, therefore, withdrew to a secluded place in the woods and waited for night.

This was trying to a painful degree. The weather which had been bitterly cold during the day, grew still colder, until the animals shivered as if with the ague. They were carefully tied where the trees partly sheltered them from the cutting wind and the hunters made sure their arms were ready. Then, when the sun went down and darkness crept over the snowy landscape, the men moved around so as to approach the camp from the direction opposite to that from which the Indians would naturally look for pursuit.

When close enough to catch sight of the flames among the trees, the hunters sank on their knees and crept noiselessly forward until able to gain a full view of the dusky thieves. They were surprised at what they saw. The savages had thrown some logs and stones together so as to make a couple of rude forts and had divided themselves into two parties. It was characteristic of them that they were holding a dance and feast in honor of the brilliant style in which they had outwitted the trappers forty miles away.

The scene was quite interesting, especially when our friends plainly saw their stolen animals tied near one of the forts. The sight of their property was anything but soothing to the wrathful trappers, who were resolved not to go back to their own camp without taking the horses along.

But the Crows were strong in numbers, well armed and ready to fight on the briefest notice. It would have been an act of the greatest rashness to charge upon their camp, while they were excited to an unusual degree by the rejoicing in which all took a hilarious part. The whites decided to wait several hours longer until most of their enemies would be unconscious in slumber.

All this time the weather was growing colder, and, toughened as the trappers had become by years of exposure, they suffered greatly. They dare not move about to keep up the circulation of their blood, for the slightest noise was liable to attract the suspicion of some of the Crows who might be prowling through the grove. More than once Carson feared his limbs were freezing, but he held out like the genuine hero he was, and his companions were all worthy of him.

At last the dance was over and the tired warriors wrapped

their blankets around their forms and stretched out to rest. Their manner showed they had no thought that a foe was anywhere in the neighborhood. Although such men sleep lightly, they do not remain long awake when courting sleep, and in a brief while all were unconscious except the sentinels on duty. Even they were so confident that nothing threatened, that they became less vigilant than usual.

"Sh! now is the time," whispered the youthful leader. They had decided long before upon their plan of action, so that no time was now lost in consultation. Kit and five of his men began slowly creeping toward their horses. This was anything but a pleasant occupation, for the snow, it will be remembered, was deep on the ground; but such veterans cared nothing for a trifle like that, and they speedily reached their animals.

Such an attempt is always a dangerous one, for the horse of the Indian or white hunter often proves his most skilful sentinel. He is able to detect the stealthy approach of a scout, long before the straining ear of his master can catch the slightest sound. If the beasts should become frightened by the shadowy figures crawling over the snow, they would be likely to alarm the camp; but Carson and his companions managed it so well that there was not a single neigh or stamp of a hoof.

Silently rising to their feet, they cut the halters which held the horses fast, and then, withdrawing a slight distance, began throwing snowballs at them. These feathery missiles fell among and struck against them, until, to escape the mimic bombardment they moved out the wood altogether, where they were taken charge by the others who were waiting. All this was accomplished without attracting the attention of a single Indian.

Having met with such success, common prudence and sense suggested that the trappers should make all haste to their own comfortable quarters, so many long miles away; but they had scarcely joined each other when they fell into an earnest discussion as to what the next step should be.

Some were in favor of withdrawing with the least possible delay, but Kit Carson and a couple of daring spirits were bent on going back and punishing the thieves who had given them so much trouble. As they could not be argued out of their purpose, the others, as a matter of course, agreed to give them their aid.

Three of the trappers were sent to take the recaptured animals to where the saddle horses were secured while the others advanced directly upon the Indian camp. They moved cautiously as was their custom and were almost upon the Crows, when one of their dogs gave notice of danger by a vigorous barking. On the instant, the warriors leaped to their feet and the fight opened. So many of the Indians were shot down and the advantage was so strongly against them, that the survivors hastily ran into the nearest fort, from which they returned the fire of their assailants. The latter, however, had stationed themselves behind trees, where they were safe against the whistling bullets, and in their attack they threw away very few shots indeed.

It began growing light in the east, and, as soon as the Crows discovered how few composed the besieging force, they in turn became the assailants, and rushed out of their fort with their frightful war whoops, but they were met by such a destructive fire that they scurried back again.

The second attack of the savages was so furious that the

trappers were forced to fall back, but the reserve, as it may be called, speedily joined them, and once more drove the Indians into their fort. Several of the whites had been wounded though not dangerously, and both parties having had enough of fighting, the battle ended.

CHAPTER VI.

THE BRITISH AND AMERICAN TRAPPER—HUNTING ON THE LARAMIE—THE DESERTERS—THE VAIN PURSUIT—ARRIVAL OF FRIENDS—THE RETURN JOURNEY—THE NIGHT ALARM—THE ATTACK UPON THE CAMP—PURSUIT AND RECOVERY OF HORSES.

A half century ago the vast region beyond the Rocky Mountains was comparatively unknown and unexplored. Its general features of course were understood, but the interior was like the central portion of Australia or Africa. Clarke and Lewis made their famous expedition to Oregon during the early days of the century, and helped to turn general attention in that direction. Its growth and development since then is one of the wonders of the age.

But there was one class (if the word may be used), who never hesitated to penetrate the wildest and most dangerous recesses of the far West and Northwest: those were the hunters and trappers. As we have already stated, the employees of the venerable and all embracing Hudson Bay Company ranged over British America and through Oregon, to which vast territory they possessed the clear legal right, besides which they and the trappers of the American Fur Company frequently trespassed on each others reserves, and not infrequently came in bloody collision with each other.

Far to the northward, the Indian drove his birch canoe across the silent Athabasca and Great Bear Lakes, on his way with his peltries to the distant factory or post of the Company; along the frozen shores of the lone Mackenzie (the only American river flowing into the Arctic Ocean), the trapper glided on his snow shoes, or with his sturdy dogs and sleigh, fought his way over the snowy wastes of Prince Rupert's Land; the brigades in their boats rounded the curves of the Saskatchewan, keeping time with their paddles to their own cheery songs; their camp fires were kindled in the land of the Assiniboine and they set their traps in the wildest recesses of the Rocky Mountains where the whirling snow storms almost carried them off their feet; but north of the dividing line, the hunters had little if anything to fear from the red men. Though they encountered in the loneliest and most desolate distant regions, they generally met and separated as friends. Among the perils of the trapper's life in British America was not reckoned that from the hostile natives.

It was far different within our own territory. Those who left our frontier States and pushed westward, and those who penetrated northward and eastward from the Mexican country, knew they were invading the hunting grounds of the fiercest Indians on the American continent. We have already told enough to show the intense hostility of the red men; between them and the hunters and trappers raged a war that never ceased or slackened, except when policy held it for a time in check.

The little group of horsemen, who rode out from

Independence or Westport, or who took steamer at St. Louis up the Missouri, often came back with several of their number missing. Up among the mountains, they had gone out to visit their traps and had never come back to camp. The lurking Blackfoot, or Sioux, or Crow, had aimed all too well, and, as he bounded whooping away, he swung aloft the scalp of his victim whose trapping days were ended forever.

After recovering their horses from the band of Crows, Carson and his companions returned to camp, where they remained until spring, when they cached their furs and made their way to the Laramie River on another hunting expedition. While thus employed, a couple of the men deserted taking several of the best animals. Kit Carson and a single companion were sent in pursuit, the rascals having a good day's start. A desperate fight was sure to follow a meeting between the parties, for Carson would never forgive such treachery, and the deserters were not the ones to permit themselves to be despoiled of their booty without doing their utmost to prevent it.

It was suspected that they were on their way to the place where the beaver had been cached; and disregarding the trail, therefore Carson made all haste thither. It need not be said that he lost no time on the road, but when he reached their old camp, he found the deserters had preceded him. They had stolen several thousand dollars worth of furs and departed.

Carson was more anxious than ever to overtake the scoundrels. He and his companion made diligent search, but failed utterly to find them. They were never seen or heard of again, and Carson was convinced they had fallen victims to the Indians who in turn made off with the stolen peltries.

It will be borne in mind that Kit and his friend were several hundred miles from the main body of hunters, and in one of the most dangerous countries they had ever visited. So dangerous, indeed, did they consider an attempt to return to them, that they decided not to make it, but to stay in the old camp. Inasmuch as it would be impossible to keep their presence from the knowledge of the Indians, they threw up some rude fortifications and never relaxed their vigilance. When Carson wrapped his blanket around him, and lay down to rest, he knew his companion was on guard and would not slumber. It was the same with his friend, their watchfulness undoubtedly preventing the attack which scarcely could have failed to be effectual.

It was needful now and then that one of them should venture out to procure game, but that was so plentiful that he was never compelled to go far, and he used such extreme care that he was not even so much as fired upon.

Thus the time passed, until at the end of several weeks, the hunters were surprised and delighted by the arrival of more than a dozen men on their way with a complete outfit to join the main body. Carson and his friend were glad enough to go with them and the long journey was begun. They had not gone far, when they exchanged shots with hostiles and there were almost daily skirmishes with them. By sunset they had travelled a long distance, and went into camp, feeling certain that though Indians had not shown themselves, they were in the vicinity. To prevent a stampede of their animals, the long ropes around their necks were fastened to stakes driven deep into the earth. This arrangement allowed them to graze over sufficient ground and opposed an almost insuperable obstacle to the success of the dusky thieves prowling around.

It was yet early in the evening when one of the dogs belonging to the camp began barking. A score of causes might have caused this but Carson believed the incitement in that instance was the one most dreaded. Several men were added to the guard and the rest lay down, too uneasy to gain much slumber, however.

The trappers were right in their suspicion that savages were near but they could not have failed to note what precautions had been taken by the whites against surprise and they withdrew without molesting them. The party were in a beaver country, and Carson and three of his men went up the stream some distance to learn whether it was worth their while to set the traps.

They had not been gone long when a party of Indians, who were probably awaiting such an opportunity, charged upon the camp and drove off all the loose horses. Four of the hunters instantly saddled the swiftest of those remaining and started in hot pursuit. So hot indeed was the pursuit that they speedily came up with the marauders and opened a running fight. One of the hunters was badly wounded, while a warrior was shot from his horse pitching headlong to the earth with a screech of agony. The remaining ones were pressed so hard that they were glad enough to abandon the property which came back to the rightful owners, probably before an animal was able to comprehend what had taken place.

The promptness and daring of the hunters had prevented a serious loss, and though one of their number was severely hurt, his wound was not mortal. It may be said that he suffered much but fully recovered in time. Men with such iron constitutions and rugged frames rallied from injuries that would have swept off those accustomed to less stirring lives.

Having righted matters, so far as possible, the trappers picketed their horses and awaited the return of Carson and his companions. They were much disturbed by fears for their safety, as in truth they had good cause to be.

CHAPTER VII.

AN UNEXPECTED MEETING—THE AMBUSH—A DARING AND PERILOUS RIDE—RETURN TO CAMP—DISAPPOINTMENTS—THE BEAVER.

Meanwhile the Indians made it exceedingly lively for Kit Carson and his three companions.

The latter had heard so much of the abundance of beavers in a certain section that they determined to visit it and make a thorough exploration. To do this, it was necessary to ride over a lofty Rocky Mountain peak or take many hours to pass around it. Very naturally they concluded to "cut across lots," confident of their ability to take care of themselves, no matter what danger threatened.

The ascent proved very exhausting to men and animals, for the trappers did not compel the weary beasts to bear them up the steep slope where it tired them to force their own way. They rested many times, but finally accomplished the ascent and passed over into the valley beyond. There, disappointment awaited them. The most careful search failed to show the first sign of a beaver and they had their labor for their pains. The toil of climbing the mountain peak was so severe that the hunters concluded to take the longer route home. Their steeds had been pushed so hard, that they were permitted to set their own pace on the return. This naturally enough was a deliberate walk, while their riders talked, laughed, jested and occasionally made some remark on the magnificent scenery by which they were surrounded. There was no call for haste, and they knew nothing of what had taken place in camp after their departure; otherwise, they might have felt more impatience to rejoin their friends.

All at once, the hunters descried four Indian warriors in the path in front. They were splendidly mounted, their hair ornamented with stained eagle feathers, their ugly countenances daubed with yellow, black and crimson paint, and they were fully armed. Their appearance showed they were on the war path.

Such undoubtedly being the case, a sight of the braves was a challenge to the hunters who accepted it without a second's hesitation.

Pausing not a moment to consult on their plan of action, Kit and his companions spurred their horses to a dead run, with the purpose of bringing them within range of their rifles, but the steeds of the dusky foes were fleet of foot and they sped away like the wind.

The pursuit was a furious one, until the flying fugitives shot by a hill, when more than fifty warriors similarly mounted and accoutred, dashed out to intercept the enthusiastic hunters. Just then it dawned upon Kit and his companions that the whole proceeding was a trap arranged by the Indians into which he and his friends had dashed at headlong speed.

It was in such crises that Kit Carson displayed his marvelous resources and lightning-like perception of the best course to adopt. The discovery of the ambush would have thrown almost any company of men, no matter how brave into a panic, or at least into temporary confusion which would have been equally disastrous. Most probably they would have reined up or wheeled about and fled in the opposite direction. The whole band would have dashed in pursuit and the running fight between four men and more than twelve times their number, every one of whom it is fair to presume was thoroughly familiar with the country, could have resulted in but one way. Skilled and daring as were Carson and his comrades, they could not accomplish the impossible, as they would have had to do in order to escape the yelling band behind them.

Kit was slightly in advance of the others, and he did not check his animal in the least. On the contrary, he urged him to his utmost, and the four sped straight ahead on a dead run, seemingly as if they meant to charge the entire war party.

Such, however, was not their intention: they shied off as much as they could, and, throwing themselves forward and over the side of their horses, ran the terrible gauntlet. No one of the trappers fired a shot, for if dismounted by the bullets of their enemies, each wished to have his loaded rifle in hand, with which to make his last defense.

The very audacity of the movement amazed the Indians. By the time they comprehended what the white men were doing, they were thundering in front of them. Then the warriors opened fire, and the bullets whistled about the horses and riders, who kept their steeds to the highest bent and finally passed beyond danger—their escape one of the most extraordinary on record.

The Indians did not pursue the hunters, two of whom had been struck by their bullets, and Carson and his friends drew their horses down to a more moderate pace. The great scout admitted that he was never more utterly deceived and entrapped by the red man in all his life. But he saw in the occurrence a deeper significance than appeared on the surface. The ambush into which he and his friends had been led was only a part of the campaign against the entire party, who, weakened by the absence of Carson and his companions were likely to fall victims to such a large band of warriors. Trembling with fear for their comrades, they again forced their animals to a high speed and lost no time in making their way back to camp. They found everything in good shape, much to their relief, and were not at all surprised to learn of the visit that had been made by the savages during the absence of Kit and his companions.

The wounds of the two trappers who were shot while running the fiery gauntlet, were found to be of such a serious nature that the party had not gone far when they were obliged to go into camp again. One of them especially, was in such a bad way that it was found necessary to carry him on a litter until the main camp was reached. There he was allowed to rest and everything possible was done to make him comfortable. When he had fully recovered, the entire company headed for Old Park, once famous on account of the immense numbers of beavers found there. Disappointment, however, awaited them, for other trappers had preceded them, and made such thorough work that it was useless for the last arrivals to unload and set their traps.

The party visited other sections but in every instance they appeared to be "a day too late for the fair;" the beaver runs had been worked so thoroughly by others that it was useless for them to expect success.

The beaver, as the reader probably knows, aside from its great value in producing fur and perfume, possesses a most wonderful instinct. They live in communities and prefer to build their houses by small clear rivers and creeks or close to springs. Sometimes they are found on the banks of lakes.

The dams which they construct with the skill of a professional civil engineer, are built for the purpose of making sure of a full supply of water at all times and seasons. These dams are composed of stones, mud and tree branches, the base being ten or twelve feet in thickness sloping gradually upward to the summit.

In building their dams, the beaver does not thrust the ends of the stakes into the bed of the river, but lays them down horizontally, holding them in place by piling mud and stones upon them. The logs which compose the dams are mostly from six to eight inches in diameter, though some have been found nearly two feet through. The enormous number of such logs used may be imagined perhaps, when the ponderous character of the dams is remembered, and when it is stated that some of them are more than an eighth of a mile wide. Every log, after being gnawed off the proper length, is stripped of its bark which is stored away for use as food during the winter.

The lodges of the beavers are composed principally of mud, moss and branches, circular in shape, the space within being seven feet in width and about half as high. The walls are so thick that on the outside the corresponding dimensions are nearly three times as great as within. The roof is finished off with a thick layer of mud, laid on with wonderful smoothness and renewed every year. The severe frosts of winter freeze the lodge into such a solid structure that the beaver is safe against the wolverine, which is unable to break through the wall, resembling the adobe structures found in Mexico and the Southwest. Even the trapper who attempts to demolish one of the structures finds it tiresome labor, even with the help of iron implements.

The beavers excavate a ditch around their lodges too deep to be frozen. Into this opens all their dwellings, the door being far below the surface, so that free ingress and egress are secured.

The half dozen beavers occupying a lodge arrange their beds against the wall, each separate from the other, while the centre of the chamber is unoccupied. During summer they secure their stock of food by gnawing down hundreds of trees, the trunks or limbs of which are sunk and fastened in some peculiar manner to the bottom of the stream. During the winter when the beaver feels hungry, he dives down, brings up one of the logs, drags it to a suitable spot and nibbles off the bark.

It is impossible fully to understand how this remarkable animal does its work, for as it never toils in the day time, it is out of the power of any one to watch its method.

The peculiar odoriferous substance, secreted in two glandular sacs near the root of the tail, is "castoreum," more generally known as "bark stone" among the trappers. The odor is powerful and is so attractive to the animals themselves, that the trapper has only to smear some of it near the trap which is hidden under water. Any beaver which catches the scent, is sure to hasten to the spot and is almost certain to be caught in the trap.

CHAPTER VIII.

CARSON AND TWO COMPANIONS SET OUT ON A TRAPPING EXPEDITION OF THEIR OWN—THEY MEET WITH GREAT SUCCESS—IS ENGAGED BY CAPTAIN LEE—CARSON'S PURSUIT OF AN INDIAN THIEF.

Kit Carson finally grew tired of wandering over the country without gaining sight of a beaver. He proposed to two of his companions that they start on a private expedition of their own. They were as disgusted as he and eagerly agreed to the proposition.

The employers of the men commended the enterprise of the little company and gave them their best wishes. Cordial farewells were exchanged all around, and Kit and his comrades left the camp on their perilous errand.

On this occasion, as on innumerable other ones, Carson showed most excellent judgment. His scheme was to keep entirely to the streams never once venturing upon the plains. Several advantages were likely to flow from this course. During the summer season the mountain Indians generally placed their women and children in charge of the old men and a few warriors and came down from their retreats to engage in hunting bison or in marching on the war path. Occasionally they are at peace with the Indians of the plains, which was a bad thing for the Mexican settlements, for they left a track of desolation among them.

Few of the trappers ventured far into the mountains, where game was abundant, so that Carson was confident of finding plenty of beavers. In this he was not mistaken. The fur bearing animals seemed to be overrunning the country, while the Indians acted not only as if unaware of the fact but as if entirely ignorant of the little party of visitors, who, making hay while the sun shines, were not long in finding themselves with as large a supply as they could carry home.

This was the ordeal more to be dreaded than all the others. While on their way to the beaver runs, they had nothing to do beyond taking care of themselves; but now their valuable peltries were liable to be captured by the Indians, who could compel their abandonment by pressing the owners hard.

But extreme and altogether unexpected good fortune attended them, and they reached Taos, without receiving a scratch or losing a fur. They found on arriving at that quaint town, that there was great demand for peltries and prices were correspondingly high. They sold out their stock for a very liberal price, and Kit's friend, despite his advice, went on a carousal which soon squandered all their hard earned wages. Kit himself, however, had not lost the lesson he learned under somewhat similar circumstances, and he laid away his funds, against the proverbial rainy day.

By this time the character of Carson was fairly formed. He was resolute, self reliant, sober, thoughtful, cool headed, wonderfully quick to grasp all the points of a situation, chivalrous, agile as a panther, a perfect master of woodcraft, and withal, charmingly modest.

While Carson was in Taos, waiting for some favorable opening to present itself, he met Captain Lee, formerly of the United States Army, but who was then a member of the firm of Bent and St. Vrain, engaged for so many years in furnishing supplies to those who visited the mountains and plains. Captain Lee at that time was thus employed and knowing the value of a man like Carson, he made him so liberal an offer that he accepted it on the spot.

In the Autumn of 1832, with a train of mules loaded with such goods as were needed by trappers, Captain Lee, Carson and a number of men started northward to find their purchasers. They followed the well worn mule path leading from New Mexico to California and which had been known for years as the "Old Spanish Trail."

They reached White River without mishap, and made their way down it until Green River was forded, when they struck across the country to Winty River, where they came upon a party of twenty hunters, who were engaged in trading and trapping as opportunity offered. They affiliated at once, for there is something in the presence of a common danger which draws men closely together.

The weather became very cold and snow began to fall. It was decided, therefore, to go into winter quarters near the mouth of Winty River. There they erected skin lodges, such as are used by many tribes of American Indians, and were content to wait the coming of spring.

The skill and address of Carson seemed to create a call for his services, no matter where he happened to be, and it was not long before he became involved in a most remarkable adventure.

Among the employees of the other party, was a shrewd civilized Indian, who was held in high regard by the whites on account of his native keenness, and who stood well in the confidence of his employer; but one day he disappeared, simultaneously with several of the very best horses. The circumstances were such that there could be no doubt the two occurrences were inseparably connected.

The loss was too serious to be borne, and the angered leader of the other company (though he had not the least claim upon young Carson), appealed to him to help him to recover his property. Carson said he was perfectly willing, provided Captain Lee would give his consent, and as the Captain was more willing to help his friend, he directed Carson to do as he saw fit.

The matchless hunter made sure his weapons were in the best order, and, mounting one of the fleetest horses in camp, he waved a merry farewell to his friends and galloped off. He had not ridden far when he turned off toward an Indian village, whose people were on friendly terms with the hunters, and, riding directly among the red men, whose lingo he understood, he asked for one of their bravest warriors to join him in hunting down a California Indian that had run off with their best horses.

Such a request coming from any other hunter would have received little notice; but those dusky barbarians not only knew Carson by name, but looked upon him as the greatest white warrior they had ever seen. He could have secured a score of braves had he wanted them, but he desired only one—a sinewy, daring fellow whom he knew could be relied on in any emergency. This Indian required no more time than Carson himself to make ready, and, shortly after Kit's arrival in the village, he rode forth again with his faithful friend at his elbow.

It was impossible for the thief to conceal the trail of the stolen horses and he made no attempt to do so. A slight examination showed the pursuers that it led down the Green River, the general course being such that Carson was confident the thief was making for California—a long distance away.

As the fugitive was well mounted and all his horses were fleet, and as he must have been quite certain he would be pursued, he lost no time on the road. The trail showed he was going at a full gallop, and, under the most favorable circumstances, the chase was sure to be a long one.

CHAPTER IX

A HOT PURSUIT—AN UNEXPECTED CALAMITY—CARSON CONTINUES THE CHASE ALONE—THE RESULT.

Everything now depended on speed. Not only was the dusky thief pushing his animals to the utmost, but Kit Carson knew he would give them little rest night or day. He was familiar with the route to California and the pursuit would be no child's play.

There could be no doubt, however, of the destination of the redskin, and Carson and his brave warrior were equally persistent with their horses. The ground flew beneath their hoofs. Across the stretch of prairie, along the bank of the rushing streams, around the rocks, over mountains, through torrents, they forced their way, with no thought of turning back or checking the speed of their animals. Occasionally the bright eyes of the pursuers glanced at the ground in front, when the displaced gravel or the indentation in the soft earth showed they had not lost the trail.

In this headlong fashion the friends galloped forward until they had placed a full hundred miles behind them. They were a long distance from home and camp, but in spite of the speed of the fugitive, Carson was confident they had gained considerably upon him. If everything went well, they ought to catch sight of him on the morrow. At this juncture, when the prospect was so encouraging, an unlooked for calamity occurred.

Carson's steed stood the great strain admirably, but the one bestrode by the Indian succumbed. He suddenly slackened his pace, staggered and trembled so violently, that, when the warrior leaped from his back, he saw he was fearfully ill. If he did not die, he would not recover for hours and even then could not be forced hard.

Carson contemplated the situation with dismay. He had not counted on anything like this, and the help of the Indian was beyond all price to him. He was unusually strong, active and experienced, and would not hesitate to attack any person single handed.

Seeing the condition of the exhausted steed, Kit proposed to his dusky companion that he should abandon him and continue the pursuit on foot, but the brave shook his head. He was equal to the exploit of running ten or twenty miles at a high pace, but a great deal more was likely to be required and he needed all his powers when the shock of the battle should come. He not only refused to continue the chase, but, knowing the character of the thief, tried to dissuade Carson from going further. They had certainly done all that could be asked of them and no one could find fault if, in the face of such difficulty, they should withdraw and return to their friends.

"No," said Carson, "I have set out to recover those horses and nothing shall turn me back. I am sorry to lose you, but it can't be helped; so good bye and good luck attend you."

And putting spurs to his steed, he dashed over the trail with compressed lips and flashing eye, determined on running down the fugitive if he had to follow him to the bank of the Pacific itself. This single act of the famous mountaineer shows his character in its true light.

In the first place, it must be remembered that Kit Carson was a man of slight figure and was never noted for his strength. Many of his companions were much more powerful, though none was so quick and active in his movements. His wonderful success lay in his coolness, agility, skill and bravery, which never "overleaped itself." As we have stated, he was below the medium stature, and never could have attained a tithe of his renown, had his muscular strength formed a necessary part of his requirements.

On the other hand, the Indian thief whom he was pursuing, was exceptionally powerful, athletic and one of the most desperate men on the whole frontier. He cared nothing for Carson, nor for any single member of the company he had left. He would expect pursuit and would be on the watch for it. Whenever he caught sight of those who were seeking him, he would not abandon the horses and flee. Far from it: he would stand his ground, and if his booty should be wrested from him the men who did it would be compelled to the fiercest kind of fight. He would not run from the attack of two or three persons: much less from one of the most insignificant men in the entire company.

The course of Carson illustrated another marked feature of his character—that of loyalty to his friends and resolution in carrying through any task he undertook. Where scarcely one man in a multitude would have pushed forward, he advanced without hesitation. He deliberately resolved to attack a fierce criminal who was as fully armed as he, as daring and perfect in his knowledge of woodcraft, and much his superior in strength.

Carson had proven the mettle of his steed, and he now showed him no mercy. The trail indicated he was gaining rapidly and he was anxious to force matters to an issue before night. Among the horses the Indian was running off were one or two whose endurance was less than the others. Their tardiness moderated the pace of the rest, and thus gave Kit a chance of lessening the distance between him and the fugitive.

At the end of the ten miles he scanned the ground in front, but nothing was seen of the thief or his horses; but the hoof prints were fresh and the scout knew he was closer to him than at any time since the chase began. The flanks of his steed shone with perspiration and froth, but it would not do to lag now. The lips were compressed and the gray eye flashed fire as before.

Ten more miles were speedily thrown behind him, and he knew he was not far from the dusky desperado, who doubtless was continually glancing backward in quest of pursuers; but the keen vision which swept around every portion of the visible horizon, discovered no sign of the thief.

Carson anticipated some attempt on the part of the fugitive to confuse pursuit and he, therefore, watched the hoof prints more closely than ever. The eagle eye continually glanced from the ground to the country in front, and then to the right and left. Nothing escaped his vision, but when his foamy steed had thundered over another ten miles the fugitive was still beyond sight.

"He can't be far off," was the thought of Carson, "I'm bound to overtake him before long."

At that moment, he caught sight of the Indian galloping leisurely forward, amid the stolen horses. The cunning savage, as the scout had suspected, was constantly on the alert, and detected Carson the same moment that he himself was discovered. Quick as a flash, he leaped from the back of his horses and started on a swift run for a clump of trees between him and his pursuer. The latter understood his purpose on the instant. If the Indian could secure the shelter of the grove, he would have his enemy at his mercy; for not only would he be able to protect his body, while loading and firing, but Carson himself, being in an open space, would be without the slightest protection against his deadly aim.

Carson cocked his rifle and driving his spurs into the flanks of his high spirited steed, charged at full speed for the same shelter. Whoever should reach it first would be the master.

The Indian had much less distance to run, and was as fleet of foot as a deer. He bounded forward with such tremendous strides, that while the horseman was still some distance away, he plunged in among the trees; but for the last few seconds the foes had approached each other at a terrific pace, a result that was not only inevitable, but desirable, to the pursuer.

The very second the savage arrived on the margin of the grove, he made a leap for the nearest tree from behind which he meant to shoot his enemy; but in the very act of doing so, he was smitten by his bullet. Without checking his animal in the slightest, Carson had aimed and fired.

The death screech of the savage rang out, as he leaped in the air and tumbled prostrate to the earth, killed by the shot that was unerring in its accuracy. The Indian himself was so near firing his gun, that his piece was also discharged, the ball whizzing harmlessly above the head of his pursuer. A couple of seconds delay on the part of Carson must have proved fatal to him, for the savage was a good marksman, and was standing still, with such a brief space intervening, that he could not have missed. It is hard to conceive of any escape more narrow than that of the daring mountaineer.

CHAPTER X.

CARSON RETURNS WITH THE RECOVERED PROPERTY—JOURNEY TO SNAKE RIVER—STARTS ON A TRAPPING EXPEDITION WITH THREE COMPANIONS—CARSON'S STIRRING ADVENTURE WITH TWO GRIZZLY BEARS.

Carson gathered the horses together and set out on his return. The distance was considerable and he was compelled to encamp more than once on the road, while he was continually exposed to attack from Indians, but with that remarkable skill and foresight which distinguished him when a boy, he reached home without the slightest mishap and turned over the recovered animals to their owner. Some days later, several trappers entered camp with the statement that a large body of hunters were on Snake River, a fortnight's journey distant. Captain Lee at once set out with his men and found the company who gave them a warm welcome. They purchased all the supplies Captain Lee had for sale, and then, as Carson's engagement with the Captain was ended, he attached himself to the other body. He remained, however, only a few weeks, for he saw there were so many that they could never take enough peltries to bring much money to the individual members. He decided to do as he had done before—arrange an expedition of his own. He had but to make known his intentions, when he had more applicants than he could accept. He selected three, who it is needless to say had no superiors in the whole party. The little company then turned the heads of their horses toward Laramie River.

At that day, the section abounded with beaver, and although the summer is not the time when their fur is in the best condition, the party trapped on the stream and its tributaries until cold weather set in. They met with far greater success than could have come to them had they stayed with the principal company of trappers. But they had no wish to spend the winter alone in the mountains and gathering their stock together, they set out to rejoin their old companions.

One day, after they had gone into camp, Carson, leaving his horse in charge of his friends, set out on foot to hunt some game for their evening meal. They had seen no signs of Indians, though they never forgot to be on their guard against them. Game was not very abundant and Carson was obliged to go a long ways before he caught sight of some elk grazing on the side of a hill. Well aware of the difficulty of getting within gunshot of the timid animals, the hunter advanced by a circuitous course toward a clump of trees, which would give him the needed shelter; but while creeping toward the point he had fixed upon as the one from which to fire, the creatures scented danger and began moving off. This compelled him to fire at long range, but he was successful and brought down the finest of the group.

The smoke was curling upward from the rifle of Carson, when he was startled by a tremendous crashing beside him, and, turning his head, he saw two enormous grizzly bears making for him at full speed. They were infuriated at this invasion of their home, and were evidently resolved on teaching the hunter better manners by making their supper upon him.

Carson had no time to reload his gun: had it been given him he would have made short work of one of the brutes at least, but as it was, he was deprived of even that privilege. Fortunate indeed would he be if he could escape their fury.

The grizzly bear is the most dreaded animal found on this continent. He does not seem to feel the slightest fear of the hunter, no matter whether armed or not, and, while other beasts are disposed to give man a wide berth, old "Ephraim," as the frontiersmen call him, always seems eager to attack him. His tenacity of life is extraordinary. Unless pierced in the head or heart, he will continue his struggles after a dozen or score of rifle balls have been buried in his body. So terrible is the grizzly bear, that an Indian can be given no higher honor than the privilege of wearing a necklace made from his claws—that distinction being permitted only to those who have slain one of the animals in single handed combat.

No one understood the nature of these beasts better than Kit Carson and he knew that if either of the animals once got his claws upon him, there would not be the faintest chance of escape. The only thing therefore that could be done was to run.

There were not wanting men who were fleeter of foot than Carson, but few could have overtaken him when he made for the trees on which all his hopes depended. Like the blockade runner, closely pursued by the man of war, he threw overboard all the cargo that could impede his speed. His long, heavy rifle was flung aside, and the short legs of the trapper doubled under him with amazing quickness as he strove as never before to reach the grove.

Fortunately the latter was not far off, and, though the fierce beasts gained rapidly upon him, Carson arrived among the timber a few steps in advance. He had no time even to select the tree, else he would have chosen a different one, but making a flying leap, he grasped the lowermost limb and swung upward, at the moment the foremost grizzly was beneath him. So close in truth was his pursuer that the hunter distinctly felt the sweeping blow of his paw aimed at the leg which whisked beyond his reach just in the nick of time.

But the danger was not over by any means. The enthusiastic style in which the bears entered into the proceedings proved they did not mean that any trifles should stop them. They were able to climb the tree which supported Carson, and he did not lose sight of the fact. Whipping out his hunting knife, he hurriedly cut off a short thick branch and trimmed it into a shape that would have made a most excellent shillelagh for a native of the Green Isle.

He had hardly done so, when the heads of the bruins were thrust upward almost against his feet. Carson grasped the club with both hands and raising it above his shoulders brought it down with all his might upon the nose of the foremost. The brute sniffed with pain, threw up his head and drew back a few inches—just enough to place the other nose in front. At that instant, a resounding whack landed on the rubber snout and the second bear must have felt a twinge all through his body.

Though each blow caused the recipient to recoil, yet he instantly returned, so that Carson was kept busy pounding the noses as if he was an old fashioned farmer threshing wheat with a flail.

It was a question with Carson which would last the longer—

the club or the snouts, but in the hope of getting beyond their reach, he climbed to the topmost bough, where he crouched into the smallest possible space. It was idle, however, to hope they would overlook him, for they pushed on up the tree which swayed with their weight.

The nose of the grizzly bear is one of the most sensitive portions of his body, and the vigorous thumps which the hunter brought down upon them, brought tears of pain to their eyes. But while they suffered, they were roused to fury by the repeated rebuffs, and seemed all the more set on crunching the flesh and bones of the insignificant creature who defied them.

It must have been exasperating beyond imagination to the gigantic beasts, who feared neither man nor animal to find themselves repeatedly baffled by a miserable being whom they could rend to pieces with one blow of their paws, provided they could approach nigh enough to reach him.

They came up again and again; they would draw back so as to avoid those stinging strokes, sniff, growl and push upward, more eager than ever to clutch the poor fellow, who was compressing himself between the limb and the trunk, and raining his blows with the persistency of a pugilist.

They were finally forced to desist for a few minutes in order to give their snouts time to regain their tone. The bulky creatures looked at each other and seemed to say, "That's a mighty queer customer up there; he doesn't fight fairly, but we'll fetch him yet."

Once more and for the last time, they returned to the charge, but the plucky scout was awaiting them, and his club whizzed through the air like the piston rod of a steam engine. The grizzlies found it more than they could stand, and tumbling back to solid earth they gave up the contract in disgust. Carson tarried where he was until they were beyond sight, when he descended and hastily caught up and reloaded his rifle, having escaped, as he always declared, by the narrowest chance of all his life.

CHAPTER XI.

ON THE GREEN RIVER—IN THE BLACKFOOT COUNTRY—THE BLACKFEET—AN UNWELCOME VISIT—THE PURSUIT AND PARLEY—DISSOLUTION OF THE PEACE CONGRESS.

The day was drawing to a close when Carson set out for camp, which was not reached until after dark. His companions did not feel any special alarm over his continued absence, for the good reason that they were confident he could take care of himself no matter in what labyrinth of peril he might become involved.

It was too late to send for the carcass of the elk and more than likely it had already been devoured by wolves. So the trappers made their breakfast on one of the beavers found in their traps, and went into camp to await the arrival of the main body of trappers, which Carson was confident would come that way. Some days later they put in an appearance, and the company proceeded to the general rendezvous on Green River, where were found assembled the principal trappers of the Rocky Mountains. There were fully two hundred divided into two camps. What a history could have been written from the thrilling experiences of such a body of men!

They had gathered at the rendezvous to buy what supplies they needed and to dispose of their peltries. It was several weeks before the negotiations were over, when the assemblage broke up into smaller companies which started for their destinations hundreds of miles apart.

Carson joined a party numbering about fifty who intended to trap near the headwaters of the Missouri. Hundreds of beavers had been taken in that section, but poor success went with the large band of which Carson was a member. That was bad enough, but they were in a neighborhood which, it may be said, was the very heart of the Blackfoot country, and those hostiles were never more active and vigilant in their warfare against the invaders.

The Blackfeet or Satsika today, are the most westerly tribe of the Algonquin family of Indians, extending from the Hudson Bay to the Missouri and Yellowstone. They number over 12,000 warriors about equally divided between Montana and British America. They have always been a daring and warlike people, and the early explorers of the Far West probably met with more trouble from them than from any other tribe on the continent.

Carson and his companions ran in difficulty at once. The Blackfeet seemed to swarm through the woods, and sent in their treacherous shots from the most unexpected quarters. Whoever made the round of the traps in the morning was almost certain to be fired upon. Matters became so bad that after a time the trappers decided to leave the country. Accordingly they made their way to the Big Snake River where they went into quarters for the winter. Even there they were not safe from molestation at the hands of their old enemies the Blackfeet.

One night, when there was no moon or stars, a band of

warriors stole into camp and ran off about twenty of the best horses. This outrage touched the hunters in the most sensitive part of their nature, and the truth no sooner became known than they unanimously agreed that the animals not only should be recovered but the audacious aggressors should be chastised.

Twelve men were selected for the most difficult and dangerous task and need we give the name of the youth who was made the leader?

With his usual promptness, Carson took the trail which was followed without trouble over the snow. The Blackfeet had reason to fear some such demonstration, and they hurried off with such speed that they were not overtaken until fifty miles from camp.

The situation was a novel one. The Indians had come to a halt and the horses were grazing on the side of a hill where the wind had blown away the snow. The Blackfeet had on snowshoes which gave them an advantage over the trappers. The latter galloped in the direction of their horses, the moment they caught sight of them. The Blackfeet fired at the trappers, who returned a scattering volley but no one was hurt on either side. Then followed skirmishing and manoeuvering for several minutes, without either party gaining advantage. Finally the Blackfeet asked for a parley to which the trappers assented.

In accordance with the usual custom, one of the Indians advanced to a point midway between the two parties and halted. At the same time, one of the trappers went forward, the rest of the whites and red men keeping their distance and watching them.

The Blackfoot opened business by what might be termed an apology which was no more genuine than many made by his civilized brethren under somewhat similar circumstances. He expressed great surprise to learn that the horses belonged to their good friends the trappers. They had supposed all along that they were the property of the Snake Indians whom the Blackfeet considered it their duty to despoil on every suitable occasion.

This glaring misrepresentation did not deceive the man who was acting as spokesman for his side. By way of reply, he asked that if such was the case, why had not the Blackfeet come forward on discovering their mistake, greeted their white brothers as friends and returned their property to them.

The replies were evasive and the hunters became convinced that the Indians were seeking to gain time for some sinister purpose; but a full parley having been agreed upon, both parties left their guns behind and advanced to where their representatives were holding their interview.

The Blackfeet still professed the most ardent friendship, and as an emphatic token of the same, produced the calumet and began smoking the pipe of peace. The tobacco having been lit, each took several whiffs and then passed it to his neighbor, who did the same until the round was completed. This solemn pledge of good will having been exchanged, the convention or peace congress was opened as may be said, in due and ancient form.

Carson and his companions were distrustful from the start, though it was hard for them to decide the meaning of the prolonged negotiations, since no one could see what the Blackfeet were to gain by such a course. They may have hoped to deceive the hunters and throw them off their guard, but, if such was the case, they failed.

First of all, the leading warriors indulged in several long speeches which were without point, but what was said in reply could admit of no doubt as to its meaning. The trappers understood the Blackfoot tongue well enough to make their responses models in the way of brevity and force. They said that it was idle to talk of friendship or peace until the stolen property was returned to its owners. The Indians still attempted to postpone or evade, but the complainants were in no mood for trifling and they repeated their declaration more positively than before.

The Blackfeet were much more numerous than the whites, and confident of their strength, began to bluster and to assert that whatever they did would be dictated by their own wishes and not by any fear of their visitors. Whether they desired to avoid a fight or not can only be conjectured, but they finally sent back to where the horses were tethered and caused five of the worst to be picked out and brought forward.

When the trappers inquired the meaning of this proceeding, the Indians said that it was the best they could do and the hunters must be content.

This last insult was the spark which exploded the magazine. Instantly every white man ran for his gun, and the Blackfeet did the same. A few seconds after they wheeled about and the sanguinary fight began.

Kit Carson and a companion were the first to obtain their guns and as a consequence they led the advance. Each selected a warrior who was partially hidden by the trunk of a tree. Carson was in the act of firing, when he observed that his friend was examining the lock of his gun all unmindful of the fact that one of the Blackfeet had levelled his weapon directly at his breast. On the instant, Kit changed his aim and shot the savage dead, thereby saving the life of his friend, who could not have escaped had the weapon of his adversary been discharged.

CHAPTER XII.

CARSON BADLY WOUNDED—A DRAWN BATTLE—
AN INEFFECTUAL PURSUIT—THE SUMMER
RENDEZVOUS—CARSON'S DUEL.

This act of chivalry on the part of Carson simply transferred the peril of his friend to himself, for the Indian whom he had selected for his target was carefully sighting at him, at the very moment the gun was discharged. Kit saw what was coming and bounded to one side in the hope of dodging the bullet. Quick as he was, however, he did not entirely succeed, though the act doubtless saved his life. The ball from the rifle of his adversary grazed his neck and buried itself in his shoulder, shattering the head of one of the bones.

Carson though badly hurt, did not fall or retreat. On the contrary, he tried desperately to reload his gun, but found it impossible to raise his arm. He was hors de combat beyond all question, and bleeding so fast that his weakness compelled him to lie down on the ground while the conflict went on about him. The fight was very hot for a time, the result being what may be called a drawn battle, with the advantage inclining to the side of the Indians. The trappers fell back to the safest place that presented itself and went into camp. They dared not start a fire; for they knew it would bring an attack from the Indians, but wrapping their saddle blankets around them, they bore the intense cold as best they could.

The sufferings of Carson were great. His wounds continued bleeding and froze upon the dressings, which were of the most primitive character. And yet not once through those hours of anguish did he utter a word of complaint. Many a strong man would have cried out in his agony, but one might have sat within arm's length of the mountaineer without knowing he was hurt at all.

More than that, Carson took his part in the council which was held in the cold and darkness. The conclusion reached was that the party of trappers were not strong enough to pursue the Blackfeet, and the proper course to pursue was to rejoin the main body and report what had been done. It would then be time enough to decide upon their future action.

When this programme was carried out, a larger party of hunters under the lead of an experienced mountaineer resumed the pursuit; but nothing could be found of the savages. They had utilized the grace allowed them so well that it was impossible to overtake or trace them, and the indignant trappers were obliged to submit to their loss.

The severe cold moderated, and, as spring was close at hand the hunters pushed their trapping operations along the Green and Snake Rivers, meeting with unbounded success. They gathered more peltries than they had dared to hope for, and when warm weather approached, went into quarters where they remained until the following fall, a party of traders having brought them all the supplies they needed.

The rugged constitution of Carson and his temperate habits

caused him speedily to recover from his severe wound. He again became the active, vigilant, keen witted guide and hunter who was looked up to by all as the most consummate master of woodcraft that had ever been known in the west.

Such a large party as were gathered at the summer rendezvous was certain to include many varieties of people. The frank, brave and open hearted, the sly and treacherous, the considerate and courteous, the quarrelsome and overbearing—indeed the temperaments of the individuals composing the company were as varied as it is possible to imagine.

Among them was a powerful Frenchman known as Captain Shunan. He had won his title by hard fighting, possessed a magnificent physique, was brave and skilled in the use of arms, and was the most quarrelsome individual in camp. It is impossible to picture a more irascible and disagreeable personage than Captain Shunan, who appeared to spend all his spare time in trying to provoke quarrels with those around him. Sometimes he succeeded, but more often his insolence was submitted to by men as brave as he, but who wished to avoid trouble with him.

The activity and strength of the Frenchman were so great that a skilful pugilist would have found difficulty in handling him. The only ground upon which he could be met with anything like fairness was where firearms were used.

On one of these occasions, the bully became unbearable in his behavior. He knocked down several weak and inoffensive persons, and swaggered back and forth through camp, boasting that he could trounce any one there. In the midst of his bluster, Carson walked up in front of him and said in a voice loud enough to be heard by those around:

"Captain Shunan, there are plenty here who can easily chastise you, but they prefer to submit to your impudence for the sake of peace: however, we have had enough and now I notify you to stop at once or I shall kill you!"

These were astounding words, and, as may be supposed, when uttered by a man six inches shorter and many pounds lighter than the blustering Captain, they fairly took away his breath. Carson spoke in his quiet, soft voice, as though there was not the least cause for excitement; but those who knew him, noted the flash of his clear, gray eye and understood his deadly earnestness.

Captain Shunan was infuriated by the words of Carson. As soon as he could recover himself, he turned about and without speaking a word, walked to his quarters. Kit did not need be told what that meant. He did the same, walking to his own lodge, from which he speedily emerged holding a single barrel pistol. He was so anxious to be on the ground in time, that he caught up the first weapon that presented itself.

Almost at the same moment, Captain Shunan appeared with his rifle. Carson observed him, and, though he could have secured without difficulty a similar weapon, he did not do so. He was willing to give his burly antagonist the advantage, if it should prove such. The other trappers as may be supposed, watched the actions of the two men with breathless interest. The quarrel had taken such a course that they were convinced that one or the other of the combatants would be killed. Captain Shunan had been so loud in his boasts that he did not dare swallow the insult, put on him by the fragile Kit Carson. Had he done so, he would have been hooted out of camp and probably lynched.

As for Kit, his courage was beyond suspicion. He feared no man and was sure to acquit himself creditably no matter in what circumstances he was placed. He was the most popular member of the large company, while his antagonist was the most detested; but the love of fair play was such that no one would interfere, no matter how great the need for doing so.

The duellists, as they may be called, mounted each his horse and circling about the plain, speedily headed toward each other and dashed forward on a dead run. As they approached, they reined up and halted face to face, within arm's length.

Looking his antagonist straight in the eye, Carson demanded:
"Are you looking for me?"
"Have you any business with me?"
"No," growled the savage Frenchman; but, while the words were in his mouth, brought his rifle to his shoulder, and, pointing it at the breast of Carson, pulled the trigger; but Kit expected some such treacherous act, and, before the gun could be fired, he threw up his pistol and discharged it as may be said, across the barrel of the leveled weapon.

The ball broke the forearm of Captain Shunan, at the very moment he discharged his gun. The shock diverted the aim so that the bullet grazed his scalp, inflicting a trifling wound; but the combatants were so close that the powder of the rifle scorched the face of the mountaineer.

Captain Shunan had been badly worsted, and was disabled for weeks afterward. He accepted his fate without complaint and was effectually cured of his overbearing manner toward his associates.

CHAPTER XIII.

ON THE YELLOWSTONE—REPEATED DISAPPOINTMENTS—CARSON ENTERS THE EMPLOY OF A HUDSON BAY TRADER—POOR SUCCESS—A TRYING JOURNEY—ARRIVAL AT FORT HALL—THE AMERICAN BUFFALO OR BISON.

With the approach of cool weather, preparations were made for the fall hunt. When all was ready, the trappers headed for the Yellowstone, which was reached without mishap, and they immediately set their traps. The country as a rule, was a good one for those valuable animals, but the visitors were disappointed to learn they were unusually scarce.

When it became evident that it was useless to work on the Yellowstone, they gathered up their traps and made their way to the Big Horn, but, failing again, tried their fortunes on other rivers in that vicinity with no better results.

It was while engaged in this discouraging work that they met a trader belonging to the Hudson Bay Company. He had been pushing operations in every direction, but the stories he told were of the same general tenor as those of the larger party. He had been as unsuccessful in the way of trade as they had been in catching the fur bearing animals.

The Hudson Bay trader, however, was confident he could succeed where they had failed, and he made such liberal offers to Carson that he and several of his companions accepted them on the spot.

The first point which they visited was the Humboldt River, from which had come reports of the abundance of beavers. They began near the head waters of the stream, and carefully trapped down to the Great Basin. Meeting with only moderate success, they made their way to Big Snake River. After remaining there a considerable time, the party divided, the Hudson Bay trader and his friends going northward toward Fort Walla Walla, while Carson and the larger number set out for Fort Hall.

The journey thither was one of the most distressing which Kit Carson ever undertook. The country through which most of the march led is one of the most dismal wastes on the American continent. Except in extent, a journey across it is similar to that of the parched caravans across the flaming sands of Sahara. Carson and his companions were accustomed to all manner of privations, but more than once their endurance was tried to the utmost point.

The trappers had gathered some nutritious roots upon which they managed to subsist for a time, but these soon gave out, and their situation grew desperate. When almost famishing they bled their mules and drank the warm current. They would have killed one of the animals, but for the fact that they could not spare it, and, as there was no calculating how long the others would last, they were afraid to take the step, which was likely to cripple them fatally.

This strange source of nourishment served them for the time, but a repetition would endanger the lives of their animals, who were also in sore straits, inasmuch as the grass was not only poor but very scanty. Matters rapidly grew worse, and soon became so desperate that Carson said they would have to kill one of their animals or else lie down and perish themselves.

At this trying crisis, they discovered a band of Indians approaching. Perhaps the hapless situation in which all were placed left no room for enmity, for the red men showed a friendly disposition. The high hopes of Carson and his friends were chilled when it was found that the Indians were in about as bad a plight as themselves. They had barely a mouthful of food among them, and, when besought to barter with the whites, they shook their heads. They had nothing to trade, and, while they felt no hostility toward the suffering trappers, they gave them to understand they could not afford any help at all.

But Carson had fixed his eyes on a plump old horse, and never did a shrewd New Englander apply himself more persistently to secure a prize than did he. Kit's companions put forth all their powers of persuasion, but in vain, and they advised Carson that he was throwing away his efforts in attempting the impossible.

But Carson succeeded, and when the equine was slaughtered and broiled, the trappers enjoyed one of the most delicious feasts of their lives. They filled themselves to repletion and felt that the enjoyment it brought was almost worth the suffering they had undergone to obtain it.

When their strength was recruited, they resumed their journey and a few days later reached Fort Hall. There they found abundance of food and received a cordial welcome. In a brief while they were as strong as ever and eager for any new enterprise.

Hundreds of bisons were in the neighborhood of the fort and

Carson and his friends slew them by the score. Indeed they kept the post well supplied with fresh meet as long as they remained there.

The animal almost universally known as the "buffalo" is miscalled, his correct name being the "bison," of which there are droves numbering, it is said, as high as a hundred thousand. The flesh is held in high repute by hunters, and not only is nourishing but possesses the valuable quality of not cloying the appetite. The most delicate portion of the animal is the hump which gives the peculiar appearance to his back. That and the tongue and marrow bones are frequently the only portions made use of by the hunter.

The hide answers many useful purposes. All know how much a "buffalo robe" is appreciated in wintry weather by those exposed to cold. It serves to form the Indian's tents, his bed, parts of his dress and is sometimes made into a shield which will turn aside a rifle ball that does not strike it fairly.

Hundreds of thousands of bisons are killed annually—myriads of them in pure wantonness—and yet enormous droves may be encountered today in many portions of the west, where it is hard for the experienced hunters to detect any decrease in their numbers.

Some of the methods employed to slay bisons are cruel in the extreme. Many a time a large herd has been stampeded in the direction of some precipice. When the leaders found themselves on the edge, they have endeavored to recoil; but there was no stemming the tide behind them. The terrified animals literally pushed the leaders over the rocks and then tumbled upon them. In a little while the gully or stream would be choked with the furiously struggling creatures and hundreds would be killed within a few minutes.

The bison is as fond as the hog of wallowing in mud. When he comes upon a marshy spot he lies down and rolls about until he has worn out a large and shallow excavation into which the water oozes through the damp soil. Lying down again he rolls and turns until he is plastered from head to tail with mud. Though it cannot be said that it adds to his attractiveness, yet the coating no doubt serves well as a protection against the swarms of insects, which are sometimes terrible enough to sting animals to death.

Those who have viewed the scraggy specimens in the menageries and zoological gardens would scarcely suspect the activity and power of running possessed by them. The body is covered with such an abundance of hair that it looks larger than it really is, while the legs appear smaller. But the bison not only can run swiftly, but possesses great endurance. They will often dash at full speed over ground so rough that the more graceful horse will stumble.

When wounded by the hunters, a bull will sometimes turn in desperation on his persecutor. Then, unless the horse is well trained, serious consequences are likely to follow. The plunging thrust of his stumpy horns perhaps rips open the steed, sending the rider flying over the back of the furious bison, who may turn upon him and slay him before he can escape.

This rarely happens, however, the bison being a huge, cowardly creature which prefers to run rather than fight, and a hunt of the game in these days often takes the character of wholesale butchery in which no true sportsman would engage.

CHAPTER XIV.

A STRANGE OCCURRENCE—ARRIVAL OF FRIENDS—CARSON JOINS A LARGE COMPANY—TRAPPING ON THE YELLOWSTONE—THE BLACKFEET—A DREADFUL SCOURGE—IN WINTER QUARTERS—THE FRIENDLY CROW INDIANS—LOSS OF TWO TRAPPERS—ON THE HEAD WATERS OF THE MISSOURI.

A singular occurrence took place a few nights after the return of Carson and his friends from an extended bison hunt. Their horses and mules were corralled near the post and a sentinel was on duty at all hours of the night to prevent the animals being stolen by the Indians who were always prowling through the neighborhood.

In the dim uncertain light, just beyond midnight, the sentinel saw two men walk forward from the darkness, and without any appearance of haste, let down the bars and drive out the stock. Very naturally he concluded they were his friends who intended to take out the animals to graze. As there was nothing more for him to do, he sought his quarters, lay down and went to sleep.

In the morning not a horse or a mule was to be found. The two individuals who had let down the bars and driven them out, were Blackfeet Indians, whose complete success was due to their amazing audacity. Had they shown any hesitation or haste, the suspicions of the sentinel would have been aroused, but when the truth became known, he was the most astonished man at the fort.

The hunters were in a most sorry plight, for the Blackfeet having made a clean sweep, they were without the means of pursuing and recovering their property. The parties who belonged at the fort had suffered a somewhat similar trick a short time before from the same tribe, so that only a few rickety horses remained in their possession.

Under the circumstances, the trappers were compelled to accept their misfortune with grim philosophy, and await the arrival of the rest of the party, who had promised to rejoin them after completing their business at Fort Walla Walla.

Sure enough, a few weeks later, their friends appeared and providentially indeed they brought with them an extra supply of excellent horses. The trappers were in overflowing spirits once more and soon started for the general rendezvous on Green River.

Other trappers continued to arrive for a number of days, until about all that were expected had come in. Trade and barter then began and lasted some three weeks. The scene was picturesque and stirring and there was much hand shaking and pleasant wishes when the time came to separate.

Kit Carson left the employ of the Hudson Bay Company trader and attached himself to a party numbering fully a hundred who had determined to trap along the Yellowstone. It will be recalled that Carson once quit a company of trappers because it was too large, and it may be wondered why he should join one that was still more numerous. The reason he did so was because they were going into the very heart of the Blackfoot country. They had suffered so much from these daring marauders that they knew there would be no safety unless they went in strong force. Furthermore, the whites had so many old scores to settle with those redskins that they meant to invite attack from them. If the Blackfeet would only offer the opportunity for battle, the trappers meant to give them their fill.

The formidable company arranged matters according to a system. Dividing into two equal parties, the duty of one was made to trap beaver, while the other furnished food and guarded the property. By this means, they would always be in shape to meet their sworn foes, while the real business which brought them into the country would not be neglected.

The hunters were confident they would not be left alone very long. The Blackfeet would resent the invasion of their hunting grounds, and to say the least, would take measures to prevent the time hanging heavily on the hands of the pale faces.

But, to the astonishment of the trappers, the days passed without bringing a glimpse of the savages. No hostile shot awoke the impressive stillness of the wilderness. Could it be the Blackfeet were seeking to throw the whites off their guard? Did they expect to induce a degree of carelessness that would enable the Blackfeet to gather their warriors and overwhelm them before they could reply?

It was not reasonable to suppose that the sagacious tribe held any such belief, for they could not have failed to know that any such hope was idle.

But the explanation came one day by a party of friendly Crow Indians, who stated that the small pox was raging with such awful virulence among the Blackfeet that they were dying by hundreds and thousands. Indeed, the havoc was so dreadful that there was reason to believe the whole tribe would be swept away.

It would not be the first time that such an annihilation has taken place among the American Indians. The treatment required by that frightful disease is precisely the opposite of that which the red man in his ignorance pursues. When small pox breaks out among them, therefore, the mortality becomes appalling.

The Crow Indians affiliated with the trappers and guided them to a secluded valley, where they established themselves for the winter. The lodges were made strong and substantial, and it was fortunate that such precautions were taken, for the winter proved one of the severest known for many years. With their abundance of fuel, they kept enormous fires going and passed the days and nights in comparative comfort.

But it was far different with their stock. During the severe weather, the only food that could be obtained was the bark of the cottonwood. The inner lining of this is quite palatable to animals and in cases of extremity it affords temporary sustenance to men. With its help actual starvation was kept away, though it came very close.

Unusual weather always brings unusual experience, and the intense cold developed an annoyance to the trappers upon which they had not counted. The difficulty of finding food was felt by the wild animals as well as domestic, and the bisons became desperate. When they saw the horses eating their fodder, they rushed forward and with lowered heads drove them away. If a horse or mule refused, he was likely to be gored to death.

The beasts finally became so numerous and fierce they would have killed all the stock of our friends if they had not kindled large fires and mounted constant guard. When the weather moderated those annoyances ended.

Had any explorer of the west found his way to the secluded valley where the trappers were in winter quarters, he would have looked upon a striking scene. The Crow Indians and white men engaged in numerous athletic sports in friendly rivalry. They maintained the best of terms, and when the bisons departed, the strange community enjoyed themselves far better than would be supposed. In truth where they were favored with such rugged health and where they had plenty of food and comfortable quarters, it would have been remarkable had they not been comparatively happy. They were not disturbed by political discussions or diversity of views on any public questions and were satisfied that the glorious Union was safe without any worriment on their part.

When spring came, two of their party were sent to Fort Laramie to procure needed supplies. They went off well mounted and armed and were never heard of again. Somewhere in the recesses of the forest or mountain, the Blackfeet had probably killed them as they had done with many a brave man before, and as they have done with multitudes since.

When it became certain the messengers had been slain, the company began the spring hunt without them. After trapping a brief while on the Yellowstone, they worked their way to the head waters of the Missouri. They met with fair success and while engaged in that section, learned that the reports of the ravages of the small pox among the Blackfeet had been greatly exaggerated. Instead of being decimated, the tribe had not suffered to any serious extent and were as strong and aggressive as ever.

The trappers were not displeased to learn that such was the case, for they desired a settlement of accounts with them. Under such circumstances it was impossible that hostilities should be long delayed.

CHAPTER XV.

A FIERCE BATTLE WITH THE BLACKFEET—DARING ACT OF KIT CARSON—ARRIVAL OF THE RESERVES AND END OF THE BATTLE.

When near the head waters of the Missouri, the trappers discovered they were approaching the principal village of the Blackfeet. They determined to attack and punish the Indians who had caused them so much trouble and suffering; but the whites were so numerous and powerful that extreme care was necessary to prevent their presence becoming known.

When a number of miles from the village, the trappers came to a halt, and Kit Carson with several men was sent forward to reconnoitre. With extreme caution they made their way to a point from which they could overlook the village.

A glance showed the Indians hurriedly making ready to move elsewhere. The shrewd red men had discovered their danger before their enemies caught sight of them. Carson galloped back as rapidly as he could, and made known what had been seen. A council was hastily called and about half the company advanced to give the Blackfeet battle. Kit Carson, as might be supposed, was made the leader. The others were to guard the property, advance slowly and act as reserve, which could be hurried forward should it become necessary.

As agreed upon, Kit Carson galloped ahead, and the moment his men came in sight of the village, they dashed through it, killing a number of warriors. The others slowly fell back, fighting as they went, and without showing the least panic. They received charge after charge of the white men, with the steadiness of veterans. By and by the eagerness of the trappers reduced their ammunition and their firing became less destructive. The Blackfeet were quick to perceive the cause, and in turn they charged upon their assailants who became immediately involved in a desperate hand to hand fight. It was then the small arms in the possession of the whites played their part. They were used with such effect, that the fierce warriors were compelled once more to retreat.

But the courageous red men recoiled a short distance only, when they halted and then, with exultant yells, dashed toward the trappers, who despite all they could do, were forced back until it looked as if the whole party would be overwhelmed and destroyed.

On this retreat, one of the horses belonging to the hunters was shot, and plunged to the ground so suddenly that his rider was caught before he could spring from the saddle. Several of the warriors were quick to perceive his sore straits, and dashed toward him, eager to secure his scalp. The poor fellow struggled desperately, but could not extricate himself, and his expression of horrified despair when he perceived the fierce red men running a race with each other to reach him, would have melted the heart of almost any one.

Carson was several rods distant, but seeing the danger of his friend, he bounded out of his saddle, and shouted to the others to rally to the defence of their imperilled comrade. Kit raised his rifle while on the run and shot the leading warrior dead. The other whites were so close behind that the remaining Blackfeet whirled and ran for their lives. Several of them were shot down before they could reach the shelter of the rocks from behind which they sprang after the fallen white man.

Carson's devotion to his friend now placed him in an unpleasant if not dangerous situation. His steed being without restraint, galloped off beyond his reach, and the commander was thus left on foot, when there was urgent need that he should be mounted.

Meanwhile the mountaineer who was caught under the body of his horse, was struggling desperately to withdraw his imprisoned leg, for there was no saying when the Blackfeet would be upon him again. He succeeded at last, and, standing upon his feet, shook himself together, as may be said, and he found that though pretty badly bruised, no bones were broken, and he was able to do his full part in the serious duty before him.

The exciting episode benefited the trappers in one respect: it served to check the seemingly resistless rush of the Blackfeet and gave the others a chance to rally and fix upon some course of action.

Carson ran rapidly toward the nearest horseman and sprang upon the back of his animal behind him. The steed was forced to his best and speedily joined the main body a short distance off. It was fortunate that just at that moment there came a lull in the furious fighting, else Carson could scarcely have escaped so well. The runaway horse was pursued by one of the mountaineers who finally cornered and brought him back to their leader.

The Blackfeet did not follow the whites, nor did the latter return to their charge against them. Both parties had gained a thorough taste of each other's mettle, and the conclusion reached was like that of two trained pugilists—their strength was so nearly equal that neither could afford to throw away his advantage by leading in the assault.

Undoubtedly Carson and his men would have withdrawn but for the hope that the reserves were close at hand. The trappers had fought valiantly but not more so than the Indians, who still possessed plenty ammunition while that of the whites was nearly exhausted. Had they advanced and encountered the warriors again, the latter would have swept everything before them. As it was, the mountaineers were by no means safe even when acting on the defensive. If the red men should charge upon them with their old time fierceness, it was by no means certain they would not destroy the whites. The fight would necessarily be of the most sanguinary nature, but when guns and small arms were useless for lack of ammunition, nothing short of a miracle could save them from annihilation.

Several hours had gone and Carson and his men wondered what could delay the reserves. Time always passes slowly to those in waiting, and to some of the hunters the tardiness of their friends was unaccountable. Carson was on the point of sending messengers back to hurry them forward, when the whole party appeared and the situation changed.

But those who expected the Blackfeet to flee in panic when they observed the doubling of the assailing forces, were much mistaken. The feeling among the Indians could not be described as in the least "panicky." They quietly surveyed the new arrivals and prepared with the coolness of veterans for the conflict that was sure to come, within the next few minutes.

The powder was distributed among the trappers, who were more eager than ever to attack their old enemies, who were as ready as they for the conflict. Nearly two hundred yards separated the combatants, when the mountaineers, leaving their horses behind, advanced on foot. The Blackfeet stationed themselves behind rocks and trees and defiantly awaited the attack.

In a few minutes the most savage fight of the day was raging. A hundred rifles were flashing in every direction and the yells of the red men mingled with the shouts of the excited mountaineers.

As the warriors had used every means to shelter themselves, it was necessary to dislodge them before they could be driven back. Without remaining together in a compact mass, the trappers made for them with the fierceness of tigers.

The result of this charge were a number of remarkable combats. A hunter would dash at a warrior crouching behind some rock, and the two would begin dodging, advancing, retreating, firing, striking and manoeuvering against each other. Sometimes one would succeed and sometimes the other. The Blackfoot, finding the situation becoming too hot, would break for other cover and probably would be shot on the run or would escape altogether. Again, it would be the white man who would be just a second too late in discharging his gun and would pay the penalty with his life.

At last the Indians began falling back and the mountaineers pushing them hard, they finally broke and fled in a wild panic, leaving many dead behind them. On the part of the trappers three had been killed and quite a number badly wounded.

the main body of trappers on Green River. All meeting at the general rendezvous on a branch of the Wind River. Still later, the majority of the trappers went into winter quarters on the Yellowstone. They were again in the country of their bitter enemies, the Blackfeet, and were certain of a fight with them; but several months passed without molestation.

One day, however, several of the trappers who were making the rounds of the traps, came upon signs which showed they were close to a strong force of the Blackfeet. The men lost no time in hurrying back to camp with the news, where it was agreed that trouble was at hand.

Forty men were selected at once to hunt out the Indians and engage them in battle. It goes without saying, that Kit Carson was made the leader and there was not a moment's unnecessary delay in starting out to find the enemy.

They were successful in their search. They suddenly found themselves in the presence of a scouting party, who were undoubtedly looking for them; but perceiving the strength of the whites, they began retreating. Carson and his men pressed them hotly, when, as anticipated, they fell back on the main body and one of the old fashioned battles between trappers and Indians began.

The Blackfeet always fight bravely, and, for a time, they held their ground well, but they were forced to give way and retired to a small island in the Yellowstone, where they had thrown up rude fortifications and felt able to hold their own against a much superior force.

Darkness closed in upon the contending forces, and the assailants ceased firing and encamped for the night on the bank of the river. They were on the qui vive through the still hours, and so eager for the attack that with the earliest streakings of light in the east, they plunged into the stream and made for the barricades. It was not to be supposed that the Blackfeet would be taken off their guard, and the trappers expected to reach the defences through a hot fusillade from the dusky defenders.

To their surprise, however, not a single gun was discharged and they rushed pell mell over the rugged fortifications to engage the enemy in hand to hand conflict. To their chagrin, however, not a solitary Blackfoot was visible. Despite the watchfulness of the white men, the entire Indian force had withdrawn during the night without arousing the least suspicion on the part of the watchers.

But the trappers were too wise to misconstrue the action of the Blackfeet. Their withdrawal was a strategic movement, and did not by any means signify they were afraid of the large force or that they would prefer not to molest them. The signs around the fortifications showed that the Indians had suffered severely and they would never content themselves until full retaliation had been made.

The trappers returned to camp, where a long council was held. The conclusion was that the Blackfoot village was near by, and when they learned of the severe punishment received by the scouting party, they would lose no time in entering upon a campaign of revenge. As the Blackfeet nation included several thousand warriors, there was reason to fear they would overwhelm the trappers, despite their bravery and skill. Barricades were thrown up and the best men stationed as sentinels. One of them hastened to the top of an adjoining hill, which commanded an extensive view of the surrounding country.

The sentinel had been in position but a short time when he

signalled to his friends the approach of a large body of Indians. The hunters immediately began strengthening their defences, and before the redskin arrived, they had rendered their position almost impregnable against any force that could be gathered in the country.

As the Blackfeet approached, the sentinel hurried down from the hill and joined the main body. Shortly after, the advance party of Blackfeet came in sight and made a reconnaissance which apprised them of the nature of the defences. They did not fire a shot but waited until the arrival of the main band.

When that came in sight, it was enough to strike dismay into every heart. There were few if any less than a thousand warriors. Dr. Peters, the biographer of Carson, says:

"It was a sight which few white men of the American nation have looked upon. Arrayed in their fantastic war costume and bedaubed with paint, armed with lances, bows and arrows, rifles, tomahawks, knives, etc., some mounted and some on foot, they presented a wild and fearful scene of barbaric fancy.

"Soon after their last company had reported, the frightful war dance, peculiar to the American savages, was enacted in sight of the trappers' position. The battle songs and shouts which accompanied the dance reached the ears of the whites with fearful distinctness. Any other than hearts of oak with courage of steel would have quailed before this terrible display of savage enmity and ferocity. This dance, to men well skilled in the ways of the Indian warrior, was a sure signal that the next day would be certain to have a fearful history for one party or the other and doubtless for both. The odds, most assuredly, were apparently greatly in favor of the savage host and against the little band of hardy mountaineers."

CHAPTER XVII.

THE MORROW—WITHDRAWAL OF THE INDIAN ARMY—AT FORT HALL—IN THE BLACKFOOT COUNTRY—THE AMBUSH—THE TRAPPERS DECIDE TO WITHDRAW—TRAPPING IN OTHER LOCALITIES—CARSON DECIDES TO ABANDON THE BUSINESS—VISITS BENT'S FORT WHERE HE SERVES AS HUNTER FOR EIGHT YEARS.

Having gone through what the red men consider the necessary preliminaries of such a grand campaign, the vast number of warriors awaited the dawn that was to witness the annihilation of the entire force that had dared to venture upon their hunting grounds without so much as asking permission.

It was scarcely light when the imposing array advanced upon the mountaineers, who coolly awaited their approach. When the Blackfeet came close enough to see the fortifications thrown up by the whites, they were astonished. They knew from previous experience the strength of such means of defence and suddenly lost their eagerness to make the attack.

After a full survey of the work before them, they concluded the task was beyond accomplishment. The magnificent force, therefore, began withdrawing. It was the turn of the trappers to feel disappointed. They had not thought of any such issue and were enraged. They shouted and made tantalizing gestures to the Blackfeet, in the hope of goading them to stand their ground, but they were too wise to do so. They retreated to a safe point where a council of war was held. It was not to be expected that after such an abrupt withdrawal, they could summon enough courage to make the assault.

When the conference was over, the Indian army, as it may be called, broke into two divisions, one of which went back toward their own village while the other set their faces toward the Crow country. Uncertain whether they would not reappear when they believed there was hope of surprising the mountaineers, the latter maintained their vigilance day and night.

It may have been that the red men made several reconnaissances, but, if so, they concluded it would be imprudent to attack the mountaineers who held their position and continued trapping as opportunity presented through the winter.

After trapping in various localities, Kit Carson and several friends visited Fort Hall, where they joined a party in the employ of the Northwest Fur Company. They trapped around the head of Salmon River and other streams, and finally returned to Fort Hall, where the peltries were sold for a fair valuation. Then Carson and a few others set out to join a party which he knew was trapping in the Blackfoot country. Upon coming up with them, he was told that they had had several sharp skirmishes with the Indians, in one of which a trapper was severely wounded. The following morning, Carson and his comrades parted from the rest and were trapping slowly up stream, when they were fired upon by Blackfeet and compelled to retreat. They hurried back and succeeded in escaping a serious danger; but the pursuit was so close that Carson hastily stationed his men in ambush. A hot fire dropped several of the warriors and caused the others to hesitate.

The halt was just long enough to allow the trappers to reload their pieces, when the Blackfeet made a fiercer rush than before; but with that pertinacious courage for which the tribe is noted, they kept up the fight through the rest of the day, determined to throw away no advantage they might gain. Had Carson chosen his position with less judgment, he and his command must have been overwhelmed, for nothing could have exceeded the daring of their assailants, who in their desperation set fire to the thicket in which the mountaineers had ensconced themselves; but the shrubbery was too green to burn well, and, after a little while, it died out. Then it must have been the red men concluded it was useless to strive further, and, learning that the main body of the trappers were not far off, they departed.

The annoyance from these Indians was so great that it was decided to leave the country. While the trappers were able to hold their own against them, yet it was impossible to make much progress in taking furs, when their attention was mainly taken up in fighting the warriors, who varied their shooting by destroying the traps that were set for the beavers.

The next scene of operations was the North Fork of the Missouri where they had been engaged only a short time when they came upon an extensive village of Flathead Indians. These showed their friendliness to the trappers by sending one of their chiefs and a number of warriors who helped them hunt along the different streams.

The following spring Carson and a single companion set

their traps in the vicinity of Big Snake River. This was the country of the Utah Indians, who were well disposed towards the whites. Thus, while furs were plenty, the couple were enabled to devote their whole time to taking them, without fear of being fired upon every time they ventured out of sight of camp. As a consequence, they succeeded beyond their own expectations, and, making their way to the nearest post, sold the stock for a fair sum.

The peltries were scarcely disposed of, when Carson organized another expedition which visited the Grand River, over which they trapped until winter, when they returned to Brown's Hole, where Carson remained until spring. Then he trapped once more in the land of the Utahs and at New Park, taking their furs to the post where he was obliged to sell them for a much less sum than he had ever received before.

The transaction had an important bearing on the fortunes of Kit Carson, for it was proof of an unpleasant truth that had been forcing itself for a number of months upon him: the days of remunerative trapping were ended.

For years, the demand had been growing steadily less both in Europe and America. The ingenuity of the manufacturer showed itself in the make of cheaper substitutes, while the beavers that had been hunted so persistently were becoming scarce: there were few regions in which trapping could be pursued with any success.

Nothing could be plainer, therefore, to Carson than the fact that he must soon give up the business and engage in something else to gain a livelihood. What should it be?

Carson and several veteran trappers started for Bent's Fort, located on the Arkansas, near an immense forest of cottonwoods, known as the Big Timbers. Messrs. Bent and St. Vrain, the proprietors, no sooner learned that Carson contemplated a change of occupation, than they offered him the position of hunter for the fort, his duties being to keep it supplied with all the game that was required.

Carson was more willing to accept the offer than he would have been under other circumstances. He agreed that the large number of men should never want for animal food, and, having given his promise, he kept it most faithfully for a period of eight years.

This statement includes a great deal, for it means that his wonderful rifle brought down thousands of deer, antelope, elk and bisons; that he tramped over hundreds of leagues of wilderness; that his splendid health never failed him, and that his knowledge of the woods and its inhabitants was as full and complete as it could be.

Furthermore, it is stated by Dr. Peters, that during that entire period, not a single impatient word passed between Carson and his employers. He attended to his duties with such regularity, promptness and skill that the only comments they could make on his work were in the nature of strong compliments.

Inasmuch as we have claimed that Carson was the superior in every respect of those with whom he was associated, we must dwell for a moment on this fact. Let the reader ask himself how many cases he knows where the term of service has been so long, in which not a single unkind word has passed between employer and employee.

His occupation as hunter was not monotonous, for where there were so many to provide for, difficult and dangerous work was required and the journeys which he often made through the long stretches of wilderness were sometimes attended with much personal danger.

But the surrounding tribes, including the Arapahoes, Kiowas, Cheyennes, Comanches and others, looked upon the great hunter with affectionate admiration and no guest was more welcome and honored in their lodges than he.

CHAPTER XVIII.

CARSON VISITS HIS OLD HOME IN MISSOURI—HE GOES TO ST. LOUIS—VOYAGE UP THE MISSOURI—MAKES THE ACQUAINTANCE OF LIEUTENANT JOHN C. FREMONT—IS ENGAGED AS A GUIDE FOR FREMONT'S FIRST EXPEDITION—THE START WESTWARD—VARIOUS MISHAPS—THE EMIGRANTS—THE FALSE ALARM.

Kit Carson had left his home in Missouri when only a boy and he was now in the prime of a vigorous young manhood. The years since he turned his back upon his old home had been busy and eventful ones and now, as is often the case with those placed as was he, he longed to visit the scenes of his childhood, and to meet and shake the hands of those of his old friends who were still among the living.

In the spring of 1842, Carson went eastward with a train of wagons, carrying goods to the States. When the borders of Missouri were reached, he bade his companions goodbye and made his way back to his old home. His experience was touching. His parents were dead, the old building which would ever linger in his memory, had tumbled down and nearly every one whom he met was a stranger. The cheeks of the hardy mountaineer were wet with tears, and with a sigh, he turned his face away forever.

Carson had never seen a large city, and he made his way to St. Louis, where he spent more than a week in sight seeing. Before the end of that time, the old yearning for the mountains, prairies and streams of the West came back to him, and he engaged passage on a steamer up the Missouri.

On the same boat John C. Fremont was a passenger. He was two years younger than Carson and had been commissioned Second Lieutenant in the Corps of Topographical Engineers, in 1838. Four years later he projected a geographical survey of the entire territory of the United States from the Missouri River to the Pacific.

Carson was attracted by the fine, manly and intellectual appearance of Fremont, and, learning he was in search of a skilful mountaineer, he introduced himself, referring in a modest fashion to his experience in the west and expressing the belief that he could be of service to the explorer.

Fremont was an excellent judge of character and was favorably impressed with Carson from the first. The answers to the inquiries which he made concerning the famous guide and mountaineer, were satisfactory in the highest degree. He engaged Carson as his guide, agreeing to pay him a salary of one hundred dollars a month.

The party of explorers were mainly gathered in St. Louis. It was composed mostly of Creole and Canadian voyageurs, Charles Preuss, a learned German, a young son of Colonel Benton (which statesman was the father in law of Fremont), several other friends, including a noted mountaineer named Maxwell, who was employed as the hunter of the party.

Including the commander, the entire company numbered twenty-eight.

With this party of explorers Fremont ascended the Missouri until the mouth of the Kansas was reached, when they disembarked and made their preparations for the long and dangerous journey before them. The march westward began June 10, 1842.

The course lay along the banks of the Kansas. All the party were well armed and well mounted, excepting eight men, each of whom drove a cart, drawn by two mules. These carts contained the stores, baggage and instruments of the expedition. A number of spare horses were taken along, so as to provide against loss in that respect. In addition, they had four oxen intended to serve as a reserve in the event of provisions running short.

It was the custom to arouse the camp at daybreak and turn out the animals to graze; breakfast followed and the march was begun. The noon halt lasted from one to two hours and the afternoon's march ended a short time before sunset. The tents were then pitched, horses hobbled and turned out to graze, and the evening meal prepared. When it became dark, all the animals were brought in and picketed, the carts arranged so as to serve as barricades and guard mounted.

An Indian guide conducted the expedition for the first forty miles along the Kansas, when he departed and the responsibility was turned over to Carson. The pilot had guided the steamer out of the harbor and upon the great ocean, and henceforth the hand of Carson was to be at the helm.

The soil over which they journeyed for many miles was of the most fertile character. Numbers of Indian farms were seen, and one could not but reflect on the possibilities of the future for the red man, who should abandon war and give his energies to the cultivation of the ground.

Such an expedition could not go far without a taste of the trials that awaited them. On the second night, the four spare horses seemed to become disgusted with the whole enterprise, and turning their heads eastward started on a rapid gallop for the States. Their loss was too serious to be borne, and a number of men were dispatched in pursuit. The chase was a long one and the animals were not recovered for several hours. One of the men lost his way and was forced to spend the night on the open prairie. At midnight it began to rain, and then the exceedingly unpleasant discovery was made that the tents on which the explorers relied for protection and shelter were so thin that they were drenched as if the water came through a sieve.

The morning, however, brought clear weather and bright sunlight, and all were in high spirits. The scenery for a time was of a pleasing and picturesque character, and they pushed contentedly forward, until they arrived at the ford of the Kansas, one hundred miles from the point where it emptied into the Missouri.

The stream was found so swollen from recent rains that it could not be forded. Accordingly several of the mounted men forced their animals into the stream and swam them across to serve as guides for the rest. They succeeded quite well, excepting the oxen, which, after floundering awhile, landed on the same side from which they started. The following morning they succeeded in crossing.

Among the useful articles with which Fremont had provided

himself, was an India rubber boat, twenty feet long and five feet wide. This was very buoyant and the carts and baggage were carried over piecemeal in it, with the exception of the last two carts. Laden with these the boat left the shore but had not gone far when the man at the helm, who was exceedingly nervous, managed to capsize the craft, with all its precious cargo. The hunters were so dismayed over the prospect of losing their stores that nearly all plunged into the stream and made frantic efforts to save what they could. Several did not stop to remember that they could not swim, so that the principal efforts of some of the others were directed to saving them.

Most of the goods were recovered, but nearly all the sugar dissolved and every grain of coffee was lost. It would be hard to imagine any deprivation greater than that to which this misfortune condemned the explorers. Carson and one of the others made such strenuous efforts in the water that they were ill the next day, and Fremont remained in camp for twenty-four hours with a view of giving them time to recruit.

The journey westward progressed without any special incident. A large party of emigrants on their way to Oregon were several weeks in advance of the explorers. Bad fortune seemed to have followed them from the start, and numerous freshly made graves were seen. One of the emigrants who had been peculiarly unfortunate, came into camp with a hunter on his way home. He took charge of the letters which the explorers desired to send to their families.

The party soon reached the Pawnee country where they were forced to unusual vigilance, for those Indians have long been noted as most persistent horse thieves. Game was abundant. Large flocks of wild turkeys were found roosting in the trees along the streams; elk, antelope and deer were plentiful, and as for bisons, they were beyond all computation.

One day a member of the company happened to be riding at the rear galloped up in hot haste, shouting, "Indians!" He declared that he had seen them distinctly and counted twenty-seven. An immediate halt was called, and Carson, leaping on one of the fleetest horses, crossed the river and galloped over the prairie.

"Mounted on a fine horse without a saddle," says Fremont, "and scouring, bareheaded, over the prairies, Kit was one of the finest pictures of a horseman I have ever seen. He soon returned quite leisurely, and informed them that the party of twenty-seven Indians had resolved itself into a herd of six elk who, having discovered us, had scampered off at full speed."

CHAPTER XIX.

ON THE PLATTE—A FALSE ALARM—THE CHEYENNES—FREMONT'S ACCOUNT OF HIS BUFFALO HUNT—DIVISION OF THE PARTY—FREMONT'S JOURNEY UP THE SOUTH FORK—THE BAND OF INDIANS—ARRIVAL AT ST. VRAIN'S FORT—THE JOURNEY TO FORT LARAMIE.

Fremont and his party, after traveling something over three hundred miles from the mouth of the Kansas reached the Platte river, where they encamped in a charming place near Grand Island. The country was most beautiful, though they suffered somewhat from the violent storms which frequently broke over them.

The noon halt was made and all were lounging about the camp, when one of the men on guard called an alarm. Everybody sprang to his feet and grasped his rifle, expecting an attack from Indians. A strange wild looking company were seen approaching, but, as they came closer, they were discovered to be white men. They were a striking sight, numbering fourteen, in the most ragged and woebegone condition imaginable. They had been on a trapping expedition, but having met with nothing but disasters from the beginning, were now straggling back to St. Louis on foot.

The explorers proceeded at a leisurely pace that day and having gone into camp, observed three Indians drawing near, one of whom was a boy about a dozen years of age. They were Cheyennes that had been out among the Pawnees to steal horses, but having met with no success, were returning home. Catching sight of the white men, they unhesitatingly entered camp, confident of being treated well, as of course proved to be the case. After supper one of the warriors drew a rude but correct map of the country around them, and gave it to Fremont.

On the first of July, while riding over a delightful prairie country, on the right bank of the river, a herd of buffaloes, numbering nearly a thousand, came up from the water and began slowly crossing the plain, cropping the grass as they went. As the prairie was three miles broad only, a fine opportunity was given the hunters to charge before the animals could scatter among the hills.

The fleetest horses were quickly saddled and Carson, Fremont, and Maxwell prepared for the chase. By that time the herd was a half mile away and they did not notice the hunters until they were within three hundred yards. Then followed an agitation of the animals, quickly followed by their precipitate flight. The horses dashed after them. A crowd of bulls brought up the rear, they having stationed themselves there to defend the females. Every once in a while they would whirl about and stare, snorting at the horsemen, as if they had made up their minds to fight; but when the hunters came nigher, they turned about and plunged after the herd. Describing the exciting incident, Fremont wrote;

"In a few moments, during which we had been quickening our pace, we were going over the ground like a hurricane. When at about thirty yards we gave the usual shout and broke into the herd. We entered on the side, the mass giving away in every direction in their heedless course. Many of the bulls, less fleet than the cows, paying no heed to the ground, and occupied solely with the hunters, were precipitated to the earth with great force, rolling over and over with the violence of the shock, and hardly distinguishable in the dust. We separated, on entering, each singling out his game.

"My horse was a trained hunter, famous in the west under the name of Proveau, and with his eyes flashing and the foam flying from his mouth, he sprang on after the cow like a tiger. In a few moments he brought me alongside of her. Rising in the stirrups, I fired, at the distance of a yard, the ball entering at the termination of the long hair, passing near the heart. She fell headlong at the report of the gun. Checking my horse, I looked around for my companions.

"At a little distance Kit was on the ground engaged in tying his horse to the horns of a cow, which he was preparing to cut up. Among the scattered band at some distance, I caught a glimpse of Maxwell. While I was looking, a light wreath of white smoke curled away from his gun, from which I was too far to hear the report. Nearer, and between me and the hills, toward which they were directing their course, was the body of the herd. Giving my horse the rein, we dashed after them. A thick cloud of dust hung upon their rear, which filled my mouth and eyes and nearly smothered me. In the midst of this I could see nothing, and the buffaloes were not distinguishable until within thirty feet. They crowded together more densely still, as I came upon them, and rushed along in such a compact body that I could not obtain an entrance, the horse almost leaping upon them.

"In a few moments the mass divided to the right and left, the horns clattering with a noise heard above everything else, and my horse darted into the opening. Five or six bulls charged on us as we dashed along the line, but were left far behind. Singling out a cow, I gave her my fire but struck too high. She gave a tremendous leap and scoured on swifter than before. I reined up my horse, and the band swept on like a torrent, and left the place quiet and clear. Our chase had led us into dangerous ground. A prairie dog village, so thickly settled that there were three or four holes in twenty yards square, occupied the whole bottom for nearly two miles in length."

The stirring buffalo hunt ended, the company advanced over the prairie for more than twenty miles, and encamped on the banks of a stream, where they enjoyed a fine feast on choice bison steaks. While they were thus employed, the wolves were attracted thither by the smell of broiling meat and prowled around camp, licking their chops, impatient for the time when they would be permitted to gorge themselves upon what should be left.

For several days there was little variation in the experience of the explorers, and no special incident took place. At the junction of the north and south fork of the Platte, Fremont, who wished to explore the south branch and to secure some astronomical observations, set out with nine men intending to advance to St. Vrain's fort, where he was hopeful of obtaining some mules. The rest of the party followed the north fork to fort Laramie, where it was agreed they would wait for the others to join them.

Fremont's experience in going up the south branch was in strong contrast to the pleasant scenes of the previous. It was midsummer and the weather was suffocatingly hot. Fierce storms of wind and gusts of rain swept the country, while the bisons were everywhere. They literally numbered hundreds of thousands, and, look in whatsoever direction the men chose, they were sure to see the huge creatures cropping the grass or lumbering across the prairie.

On the fourth day a band of three hundred mounted Indians suddenly appeared. The chief proved to be an old acquaintance of Maxwell and showed genuine pleasure in meeting him. They shook hands and the sachem conducted the little party to his village, where they received most hospitable treatment.

Resuming their journey, they encamped in a cottonwood grove in a chilly drizzling rain. The next morning dawned bright and clear, and they caught their first glimpse of the Rocky Mountains. They gazed long on the snowy peaks outlined in the far distance like fleecy clouds against the blue sky.

St. Vrain's Fort was reached on the tenth day. They were made welcome by Mr. St. Vrain, who was much interested in the expedition westward and did everything he could to assist Lieutenant Fremont in the enterprise. The needed horses and mules were secured, and three men were hired to accompany them across the country to Fort Laramie.

This station was a hundred and twenty-five miles distant, and the new hands engaged, as a matter of course, were so familiar with it, that there was no possibility of going astray. The journey was resumed on the second day after reaching the fort, and without meeting with any particular incident they arrived at their destination, three days later.

Fort Laramie, at that time, was one of the most important posts of the far west. It had large bastions at the corners, and its high walls were whitewashed and picketed.

Several lodges of Sioux Indians were pitched close by, and the division under charge of Kit Carson having arrived several days before, had also gone into camp with the appearance of the commander of the expedition.

CHAPTER XX

ALARMING NEWS—FREMONT PRESSES FORWARD AND IS NOT MOLESTED—ARRIVAL AT SOUTH PASS—FREMONT'S ACCOUNT OF THE ASCENT OF THE HIGHEST PEAK OF THE ROCKY MOUNTAINS—THE RETURN TO FORT LARAMIE—CARSON STARTS FOR NEW MEXICO—END OF FREMONT'S FIRST EXPLORING EXPEDITION.

Alarming news awaited Fremont at Fort Laramie. A number of trappers informed them that the Sioux, through whose country their route lay, were excited to exasperation by several recent conflicts with hunters in which the red men were worsted. The Sioux warriors were gathered in large numbers and would attack any white men who ventured beyond the fort. They had already massacred a number and it was impossible for Fremont and his party to get through without a battle in which they were likely to be overwhelmed.

Carson looked upon the situation as so serious that he made his will and left it at the fort. When consulted by Fremont, he said he considered the prospect full of peril, but he was ready to go the moment required. The commander was confident the danger was greatly exaggerated, and, without much misgiving, he resumed his journey westward, following up the north fork of the Platte. Game and water were found, and, at the end of three weeks, they arrived at the South Pass of the Rocky Mountains without having exchanged a shot with a red man on the way.

They had now reached their destination and Lieutenant Fremont at once began his observations. When they were concluded he undertook the ascent of the highest mountain peak. The situation was anything but encouraging: they were in the country of the hostile Blackfeet, some of whom were observed hovering in the vicinity; men and animals were worn out and it was hard to procure game. But the ascent was begun, Fremont taking fourteen men with him. Those who were left in camp erected a rude but strong fort, behind which they were confident they could sustain themselves against any force the Indians were likely to muster.

The ascent of the mountain was laborious in the extreme. Kit Carson climbed to one of the loftiest peaks from which he gained a full view of the very highest elevation. The next day Fremont sent Carson and several of the men back. He unquestionably intended that no one should share with him the honor of climbing the most elevated point. This exploit is worthy of description at the hands of the Pathfinder himself.

"At intervals we reached places where a number of springs gushed from the rocks, and about 1,800 feet above the lakes came to the snow line. From this point our progress was uninterrupted climbing. Hitherto, I had worn a pair of thick moccasins, with soles of parfleche but here I put on a light thin pair, which I had brought for the purpose, as now the use of our toes became necessary to a further advance. I availed myself of a sort of comb of the mountain, which stood against the wall like a buttress, and which the wind and solar radiation, joined to the steepness of the smooth rock, had kept almost entirely free from snow. Up this I made my way rapidly. Our cautious method of advancing in the outset had spared my strength; and, with the exception of a slight disposition to headache, I felt no remains of yesterday's illness. In a few minutes we reached a point where the buttress was overhanging, and there was no other way of surmounting the difficulty than by passing around one side of it, which was the face of a vertical precipice of several hundred feet."

Parfleche is the name given to buffalo hide. The Indian women prepare it by scraping and drying. It is exceedingly tough and hard, and receives its name from the circumstance that it cannot be pierced by arrows or spears.

The entire dress of Fremont and his party, on their ascent to the "top of America," consisted of a blue flannel shirt, free and open at the neck, the collar turning down over a black silk handkerchief tied loosely, blue cloth pantaloons, a slouched broad brimmed hat, and moccasins as above described. It was well adapted to climbing, quite light, and at the same time warm, and every way comfortable.

"Putting hands and feet in the crevices between the blocks, I succeeded in getting over it, and when I reached the top, found my companions in a small valley below. Descending to them, we continued climbing, and in a short time reached the crest. I sprang upon the summit and another step would have precipitated me into an immense snow field five hundred feet below. To the edge of this field was a sheer icy precipice; and then, with a gradual fall, the field sloped off for about a mile, until it struck the foot of another lower ridge. I stood on a narrow crest about three feet in width, with an inclination of about 20 degrees N. 51 degrees E. As soon as I had gratified the first feelings of curiosity I descended, and each man ascended in turn, for I would only allow one at a time to mount the unstable and precarious slab, which it seemed a breath would hurl into the abyss below. We mounted the barometer in the snow of the summit, and, fixing a ramrod in a crevice, unfurled the national flag, to wave in the breeze, where never flag waved before. During our morning's ascent, we met no sign of animal life, except a small bird having the appearance of a sparrow. A stillness the most profound, and a terrible solitude forced themselves constantly on the mind as the great features of the place. Here, on the summit, where the stillness was absolute, unbroken by any sound, and the solitude complete, we thought ourselves beyond the region of animated life; but while we were sitting on the rock, a solitary bee (bombus terrestris, the humble bee) came winging his flight from the eastern valley, and lit on the knee of one of the men.

"Around us the whole scene had one main striking feature, which was that of terrible convulsion. Parallel to its length, the ridge was split into chasms and fissures, between which rose the thin, lofty walls, terminated with slender minarets and columns, which are correctly represented in the view from the camp on Island Lake. According to the barometer, the little crest of the wall on which we stood was three thousand five hundred and seventy feet above that place, and two thousand seven hundred and eighty feet above the little lakes at the bottom, immediately at our feet.

"Our camp at the Two Hills (an astronomical station) bore

south 30 east, which, with a bearing afterward obtained from a fixed position, enabled us to locate the peak. The bearing of the Trois Tetons was north 50 degrees west, and the direction of the central ridge of the Wind River Mountains south 39 degrees east. The summit rock was gneiss. Sienite and feldspar succeeded in our descent to the snow line, where we found a felspathic granite. I had remarked that the noise produced by the explosion of our pistols had the usual degree of loudness, but was not in the least prolonged, expiring almost instantaneously. Having now made what observations our means afforded, we proceeded to descend. We had accomplished an object of laudable ambition, and beyond the strict order of our instructions. We had climbed the loftiest peak of the Rocky Mountains and looked down upon the snow a thousand feet below, and, standing where human foot had never stood before, felt the exultation of first explorers. It was about two o'clock when we left the summit; and when we reached the bottom the sun had already sunk behind the wall, and the day was drawing to a close. It would have been pleasant to linger here and on the summit longer; but we hurried away as rapidly as the ground would permit, for it was an object to regain our party as soon as possible, not knowing what accident the next hour might bring forth."

This mountain which bears the name of Fremont's Peak, in honor of the great Pathfinder, was found to be 13,570 feet above the Gulf of Mexico.

The object of the expedition was accomplished and preparations were made for the return to the states. No accident worth the mention had befallen the explorers, and the Blackfeet, from whom so much was feared, did not molest them. It may have been that when their scouts reconnoitred the camp, they found the barricades so strong and the garrison so watchful that they decided it would be too costly to make an attack upon them. It is not impossible that some one or more of them recognized the daring mountaineer who more than once years before had given their warriors such severe defeat and punishment. If such was the truth, we cannot but respect the discretion they showed.

Fort Laramie was reached in the month of September 1842. There as Kit Carson's labors were ended, he bade his commander and friends goodbye and started for New Mexico. Fremont and his men reached the states in safety and thus ended his first exploring expedition.

CHAPTER XXI.

CARSON STARTS FOR THE STATES—THE ENCAMPMENT OF CAPTAIN COOK AND HIS DRAGOONS—CARSON UNDERTAKES A DELICATE AND DANGEROUS MISSION—THE PERILOUS JOURNEY—RETURN OF CARSON AND THE MEXICAN BOY—ENCOUNTER WITH FOUR UTAH INDIANS—ARRIVAL AT BENT'S FORT.

Early in the year 1843, Kit Carson married his second wife and shortly after agreed to accompany an expedition of Bent & St. Vrain's wagons to the States. When part way across the plains, they struck the old Santa Fe trail and came upon an encampment of Captain Cook with four companies of United States Dragoons.

They were engaged in escorting a train of Mexican wagons to the boundary line between New Mexico and the United States. The train was a very valuable one and an escort of a hundred men were hired to accompany it through the Indian country.

The situation of this train was an alarming one. It was the duty of Captain Cook and his soldiers to guard it as far as the fording of the Arkansas, at that time the boundary line between the two countries. There was good reason for believing that a strong band of Texan rangers were waiting beyond, with the intention of attacking and plundering the train. Indeed the Mexican who had it in charge had received information that left no possible doubt of the fact.

His face lighted up when he recognized Kit Carson. Hardly waiting until they had greeted each other, he offered him a liberal reward if he would ride post haste to Santa Fe and deliver a letter to the Governor, containing an urgent request to send a strong force to escort the train thither.

Carson unhesitatingly accepted the offer and with his usual promptness started almost immediately on his delicate and dangerous business. The journey was one of several hundred miles through a country swarming with Indians, and all the skill, cunning and vigilance of the great scout would be required to succeed. But he never faltered in the face of peril.

A veteran mountaineer agreed to keep him company, but, when Bent's Fort was reached he refused to go further, and Carson, as he had often done before in critical situations, went on alone.

The news which he heard at the fort was of a startling nature. The Utah Indians were hostile and his long journey led him directly through their country. He could not censure his friend for declining to go further, nor could he blame others whom he asked to accompany him, when they shook their heads. Mr. Bent understood the peculiar danger in which Kit would be placed, and though he was splendidly mounted, he loaned him a magnificent steed which he led, ready to mount whenever the necessity should arise for doing so.

That journey was one of the most remarkable of the many made by Kit Carson. It would have been less so, had he possessed a companion of experience, for they could have counselled together, and one would have kept watch while the other slept. As it was, Carson was compelled to scan every portion of the plain before him, on the constant lookout for Indians, who would have spared no effort to circumvent and slay him, had they known of his presence in their country. He was so placed, indeed, that only by the most consummate skill could he hope to run the continuous gauntlet, hundreds of miles in length.

He had gone but a short distance when he detected the trails of his enemies, showing they were numerous and liable to be encountered at any moment. When night came, he picketed his horses and lay down on the prairie or in some grove, ready to leap to his feet, bound upon one of his steeds and gallop away on a dead run. Where the hunter has no friend to mount guard, he is often compelled to depend upon his horses, who frequently prove the best kind of sentinels. They are quick to detect the approach of strangers, and a slight neigh or stamp of the foot is enough to give the saving warning.

A large portion of the country over which he rode, was a treeless plain and the keen blue eyes of the matchless mountaineer were kept on a continual strain. A moving speck in the distant horizon, the faint column of thin smoke rising from the far off grove, or a faint yellow dust against the blue sky, could only mean one thing—the presence of enemies, for he was in a region which contained not a single friend.

One afternoon Carson discovered an Indian village directly ahead of him and on the trail which he was following. He instantly withdrew beyond sight of any who might be on guard, and, hunting a sparse grove of timber, kept within it until dark; then he made a long circuit, and came back to the trail far beyond it. He travelled a long distance that night and by daylight was in no danger of detection.

By using such extreme caution and watchfulness, he succeeded in passing the entire distance without exchanging a hostile shot with anyone. He reached Taos, where he waited as agreed upon, until his message could be sent to the Governor at Santa Fe. While in Taos he learned that one hundred men had been sent out to meet the caravan and the Governor himself was about ready to follow with six hundred more. It may be stated in this place that the smaller company, while looking for the train was attacked by the Texan rangers and with a single exception every man was killed; but venturing into American territory, the rangers were disarmed by Captain Cook and his dragoons, and the wealthy wagon train, with its valuable cargo reached its destination in safety.

Having accomplished his mission, Carson set out on his return to Bent's Fort. This time he took a Mexican boy with him. The mountaineer had become strongly attached to the youth, who was a noble, high minded lad, the fit companion of the prince among plainsmen.

Two days out from Taos, both were surprised to find themselves confronted by four Utah Indians on the war path. They appeared so suddenly, that the two friends were given little time to make preparation; but, as some distance separated the parties, Kit and the lad hastily consulted over what was best to do.

"It is you whom they are seeking," said the youth, "and your life is worth a great deal more than mine; you have a swift horse; mount him and dash off; perhaps they will spare me, but you cannot help me by staying."

"Your offer is a kind one," said Carson much touched by the words of his young friend; "but nothing in the world would induce me to leave you. We will stick together and if we must die, why let's each take a warrior with us."

The leading warrior sauntered toward the couple, while they were hastily consulting together, after the manner of one who felt he was master of the situation. A broad grin stretched across his painted face, as he extended one hand to salute Carson, while he reached for his rifle with the other. Just as his fingers were closing around the weapon of the mountaineer, the latter struck him a violent blow in the face, which sent him staggering several paces backward. The other Utahs instantly ran forward to the help of their comrade.

When they were within a few rods, Carson brought his gun to his shoulder and peremptorily ordered them to halt. They hesitated, as if uncertain what to do, when he told them that if they advanced another step or made any hostile demonstration, both he and his companion would fire. They would be sure of hitting two of the warriors, when it would become something like an even fight, with two on each side, and with the prospect that the red men might suffer still further.

But the Indians were not to be bluffed in such an easy fashion. They brandished their guns, shook powder in the pans and talked boastingly of what they meant to do. They were double the number of their enemies and they would teach them how brave Utah warriors were.

Neither Carson nor the lad was disturbed by these demonstrations, which meant to intimidate them. The mountaineer whispered to his brave young companion to keep on his guard against any sudden rush or demonstration. But the lad scarcely needed the warning. He was as alert and vigilant as his friend. Had the red men attempted anything hostile, the two would have fired instantly and then drawn their pistols and been ready for the others.

The Utahs finally saw it was useless to attempt to bluff the man and boy, and they rode away without offering them the least harm. Carson and his young companion instantly resumed their journey, still watchful and alert; but they reached Bent's Fort without molestation, and the dangerous venture was over.

CHAPTER XXII.

KIT CARSON HEARS SURPRISING NEWS—HE VISITS FREMONT—IS RE-ENGAGED AS GUIDE—FREMONT'S ACCOUNT OF HIS VISIT TO SALT LAKE.

Kit Carson was astonished on reaching Bent's Fort to learn that Lieutenant Fremont had gone by on his second exploring expedition but a few days before. Carson felt a strong attachment for his old leader and galloped nearly a hundred miles to overtake him. Fremont gave the mountaineer most cordial greeting and insisted so strongly on his accompanying him that Carson could not refuse.

The object of Fremont's second exploration was to connect the survey of the previous year with those of Commander Wilkes on the Pacific coast. The first objective point was the Great Salt Lake of Utah, of which very little was known at that time.

Carson was sent back to the fort to procure a number of mules. He did as directed and rejoined Fremont at St. Vrain's Fort. The region traversed by these explorers is so well known today that it is hard to realize what a terra incognita it was but a short time since. Perhaps it will be most instructive at this point to quote the words of the great Pathfinder himself. The party arrived on the 21st of August on the Bear River, one of the principal tributaries of Great Salt Lake. The narrative of Fremont proceeds:

"We were now entering a region, which for us possessed a strange and extraordinary interest. We were upon the waters of the famous lake which forms a salient point among the remarkable geographical features of the country, and around which the vague and superstitious accounts of the trappers had thrown a delightful obscurity, which we anticipated pleasure in dispelling, but which, in the meantime, left a crowded field for the exercise of our imagination.

"In our occasional conversations with the few old hunters who had visited the region, it had been a subject of frequent speculation; and the wonders which they related were not the less agreeable because they were highly exaggerated and impossible.

"Hitherto this lake had been seen only by trappers, who were wandering through the country in search of new beaver streams, caring very little for geography; its islands had never been visited; and none were to be found who had entirely made the circuit of its shores, and no instrumental observations, or geographical survey of any description, had ever been made anywhere in the neighboring region. It was generally supposed that it had no visible outlet; but, among the trappers, including those in my own camp, were many who believed that somewhere on its surface was a terrible whirlpool, through which its waters found their way to the ocean by some subterranean communication. All these things had been made a frequent subject of discussion in our desultory conversations around the fires at night; and my own mind had become tolerably well filled with their indefinite pictures, and insensibly colored with their romantic descriptions, which, in the pleasure of excitement, I was well disposed to believe, and half expected to realize.

"In about six miles' travel from our encampment we reached one of the points in our journey to which we had always looked forward with great interest—the famous Beer Springs, which, on account of the effervescing gas and acid taste, had received their name from the voyageurs and trappers of the country, who, in the midst of their rude and hard lives, are fond of finding some fancied resemblance to the luxuries they rarely have the good fortune to enjoy.

"Although somewhat disappointed in the expectations which various descriptions had led me to form of unusual beauty of situation and scenery, I found it altogether a place of very great interest; and a traveller for the first time in a volcanic region remains in a constant excitement, and at every step is arrested by something remarkable and new. There is a confusion of interesting objects gathered together in a small space. Around the place of encampment the Beer Springs were numerous but, as far as we could ascertain, were entirely confined to that locality in the bottom. In the bed of the river in front, for a space of several hundred yards, they were very abundant; the effervescing gas rising up and agitating the water in countless bubbling columns. In the vicinity round about were numerous springs of an entirely different and equally marked mineral character. In a rather picturesque spot, about 1,300 yards below our encampment and immediately on the river bank, is the most remarkable spring of the place. In an opening on the rock, a white column of scattered water is thrown up, in form, like a jet d'eau, to a variable height of about three feet, and, though it is maintained in a constant supply, its greatest height is attained only at regular intervals, according to the action of the force below. It is accompanied by a subterranean noise, which, together with the motion of the water, makes very much the impression of a steamboat in motion; and, without knowing that it had been already previously so called, we gave to it the name of the Steamboat Spring. The rock through which it is forced is slightly raised in a convex manner, and gathered at the opening into an urn mouthed form, and is evidently formed by continued deposition from the water, and colored bright red by oxide of iron.

"It is a hot spring, and the water has a pungent, disagreeable metallic taste, leaving a burning effect on the tongue. Within perhaps two yards of the jet d'eau, is a small hole of about an inch in diameter, through which, at regular intervals, escapes a blast of hot air with a light wreath of smoke, accompanied by a regular noise.

"As they approached the lake, they passed over a country of bold and striking scenery, and through several 'gates,' as they called certain narrow valleys. The 'standing rock' is a huge column, occupying the centre of one of these passes. It fell from a height of perhaps 3,000 feet, and happened to remain in its present upright position.

"At last, on the 6th of September, the object for which their eyes had long been straining was brought to view.

"September 6.—This time we reached the butte without any difficulty; and ascending to the summit, immediately at our feet beheld the object of our anxious search, the waters of the Inland Sea, stretching in still and solitary grandeur, far beyond the limit of our vision. It was one of the great points of the exploration; and as we looked eagerly over the lake in the first emotions of excited pleasure, I am doubtful if the followers of Balboa felt more enthusiasm when, from the heights of the Andes, they saw for the first time the great Western Ocean. It was certainly a magnificent object, and a noble terminus to this part of our expedition; and to travellers so long shut up among mountain ranges, a sudden view over the expanse of silent waters had in it something sublime. Several large islands raised their high rocky heads out of the waves; but whether or not they were timbered was still left to our imagination, as the distance was too great to determine if the dark hues upon them were woodland or naked rock. During the day the clouds had been gathering black over the mountains to the westward, and while we were looking, a storm burst down with sudden fury upon the lake, and entirely hid the islands from our view.

"On the edge of the stream a favorable spot was selected in a grove, and felling the timber, we made a strong corral, or horse pen, for the animals, and a little fort for the people who were to remain. We were now probably in the country of the Utah Indians, though none reside upon the lake. The India rubber boat was repaired with prepared cloth and gum, and filled with air, in readiness for the next day.

"The provisions which Carson had brought with him being now exhausted, and our stock reduced to a small quantity of roots, I determined to retain with me only a sufficient number of men for the execution of our design; and accordingly seven were sent back to Fort Hall, under the guidance of Francois Lajeunesse, who, having been for many years a trapper in the country, was an experienced mountaineer.

"We formed now but a small family. With Mr. Preuss and

myself, Carson, Bernier, and Basil Lajeunesse had been selected for the boat expedition—the first ever attempted on this interior sea; and Badau, with Derosier, and Jacob (the colored man), were to be left in charge of the camp. We were favored with most delightful weather. Tonight there was a brilliant sunset of golden orange and green, which left the western sky clear and beautifully pure; but clouds in the east made me lose an occulation. The summer frogs were singing around us, and the evening was very pleasant, with a temperature of 60 degrees—a night of a more southern autumn. For our supper, we had yampak, the most agreeably flavored of the roots, seasoned by a small fat duck, which had come in the way of Jacob's rifle. Around our fire tonight were many speculations on what tomorrow would bring forth; and in our busy conjectures we fancied that we should find every one of the large islands a tangled wilderness of trees and shrubbery, teeming with game of every description that the neighboring region afforded, and which the foot of a white man or Indian had never violated. Frequently, during the day, clouds had rested on the summits of their lofty mountains, and we believed that we should find clear streams and springs of fresh water; and we indulged in anticipations of the luxurious repasts with which we were to indemnify ourselves for past privations. Neither, in our discussions, were the whirlpool and other mysterious dangers forgotten, which Indian and hunter's stories attributed to this unexplored lake. The men had discovered that, instead of being strongly sewed, (like that of the preceding year, which had so triumphantly rode the canons of the Upper Great Platte), our present boat was only pasted together in a very insecure manner, the maker having been allowed so little time in the construction that he was obliged to crowd the labor of two months into several days. The insecurity of the boat was sensibly felt by us; and mingled with the enthusiasm and excitement that we all felt at the prospect of an undertaking which had never before been accomplished was a certain impression of danger, sufficient to give a serious character to our conversation. The momentary view which had been had of the lake the day before, its great extent and rugged islands, dimly seen amidst the dark waters in the obscurity of the sudden storm, were well calculated to heighten the idea of undefined danger with which the lake was generally associated."

"September 8.—A calm, clear day, with a sunrise temperature of 41 degrees. In view of our present enterprise, a part of the equipment of the boat had been made to consist of three airtight bags, about three feet long, and capable each of containing five gallons. These had been filled with water the night before, and were now placed in the boat, with our blankets and instruments, consisting of a sextant, telescope, spyglass, thermometer, and barometer.

"In the course of the morning we discovered that two of the cylinders leaked so much as to require one man constantly at the bellows, to keep them sufficiently full of air to support the boat. Although we had made a very early start, we loitered so much on the way—stopping every now and then, and floating silently along, to get a shot at a goose or a duck—that it was late in the day when he reached the outlet. The river here divided into several branches, filled with fluvials, and so very shallow that it was with difficulty we could get the boat along, being obliged to get out and wade. We encamped on a low point among rushes and young willows, where there was a quantity of driftwood, which served for our fires. The evening was mild and clear; we made a pleasant bed of the young willows; and geese and ducks enough had been killed for an abundant supper at night, and for breakfast next morning. The stillness of the night was enlivened by millions of waterfowl.

"September. 9.—The day was clear and calm; the thermometer at sunrise at 49 degrees. As is usual with the trappers on the eve of any enterprise, our people had made dreams, and theirs happened to be a bad one—one which always preceded evil—and consequently they looked very gloomy this morning; but we hurried through our breakfast, in order to make an early start, and have all the day before us for our adventure. The channel in a short distance became so shallow that our navigation was at an end, being merely a sheet of soft mud, with a few inches of water, and sometimes none at all, forming the low water shore of the lake. All this place was absolutely covered with flocks of screaming plover. We took off our clothes, and, getting overboard, commenced dragging the boat—making, by this operation, a very curious trail, and a very disagreeable smell in stirring up the mud, as we sank above the knee at every step. The water here was still fresh, with only an insipid and disagreeable taste, probably derived from the bed of fetid mud. After proceeding in this way about a mile, we came to a small black ridge on the bottom, beyond which the water became suddenly salt, beginning gradually to deepen, and the bottom was sandy and firm. It was a remarkable division, separating the fresh water of the rivers from the briny water of the lake, which was entirely saturated with common salt. Pushing our little vessel across the narrow boundary, we sprang on board, and at length were afloat on the waters of the unknown sea.

"We did not steer for the mountainous islands, but directed our course towards a lower one, which it had been decided we should first visit, the summit of which was formed like the crater at the upper end of Bear River Valley. So long as we could touch the bottom with our paddles, we were very gay; but gradually, as the water deepened, we became more still in our frail bateau of gum cloth distended with air, and with pasted seams. Although the day was very calm, there was a considerable swell on the lake; and there were white patches of foam on the surface, which were slowly moving to the southward, indicating the set of a current in that direction, and recalling the recollection of the whirlpool stories. The water continued to deepen as we advanced; the lake becoming almost transparently clear, of an extremely beautiful bright green color; and the spray which was thrown into the boat and over our clothes, was directly converted into a crust of common salt, which covered also our hands and arms. 'Captain,' said Carson, who for sometime had been looking suspiciously at some whitening appearances outside the nearest islands, 'what are those yonder?—won't you just take a look with the glass?' We ceased paddling for a moment, and found them to be the caps of the waves that were beginning to break under the force of a strong breeze that was coming up the lake. The form of the boat seemed to be an admirable one, and it rode on the waves like a water bird; but, at the same time, it was extremely slow in its progress. When we were a little more than half way across the reach, two of the divisions between the cylinders gave way, and it required the constant use of the bellows to keep in a sufficient quantity of air. For a long time we scarcely seemed to approach our island, but gradually we worked across the rougher sea of the open channel, into the smoother water under the lee of the island, and began to discover that what we took for a long row of pelicans, ranged on the beach, were only low cliffs whitened with salt by the spray of the waves; and about noon we reached the shore, the transparency of the water enabling us to see the bottom at a considerable depth.

"The cliffs and masses of rock along the shore were whitened by an incrustation of salt where the waves dashed up against them; and the evaporating water, which had been left in holes and hollows on the surface of the rocks, was covered with a crust of salt about one eighth of an inch in thickness.

"Carrying with us the barometer and other instruments, in the afternoon we ascended to the highest point of the island—a bare, rocky peak, 800 feet above the lake. Standing on the summit, we enjoyed an extended view of the lake, inclosed in a basin of rugged mountains, which sometimes left marshy flats and extensive bottoms between them and the shore, and in other places came directly down into the water with bold and precipitous bluffs.

"As we looked over the vast expanse of water spread out beneath us, and strained our eyes along the silent shores over which hung so much doubt and uncertainty, and which were so full of interest to us, I could hardly repress the almost irresistible desire to continue our exploration; but the lengthening snow on the mountains was a plain indication of the advancing season, and our frail linen boat appeared so insecure that I was unwilling to trust our lives to the uncertainties of the lake. I therefore unwillingly resolved to terminate our survey here, and remain satisfied for the present with what we had been able to add to the unknown geography of the region. We felt pleasure also in remembering that we were the first who, in the traditionary annals of the country, had visited the islands, and broken, with the cheerful sound of human voices, the long solitude of the place.

"I accidentally left on the summit the brass cover to the object end of my spyglass and as it will probably remain there undisturbed by Indians, it will furnish matter of speculation to some future traveller. In our excursions about the island, we did not meet with any kind of animal: a magpie, and another larger bird, probably attracted by the smoke of our fire, paid us a visit from the shore, and were the only living things seen during our stay. The rock constituting the cliffs along the shore where we were encamped, is a talcous rock, or steatite, with brown spar.

"At sunset, the temperature was 70 degrees. We had arrived just in time to obtain a meridian altitude of the sun, and other observations were obtained this evening, which placed our camp in latitude 41 degrees 10' 42" and longitude 112 degrees 21' 05" from Greenwich. From a discussion of the barometrical observations made during our stay on the shores of the lake, we have adopted 4,200 feet for its elevation above the Gulf of Mexico. In the first disappointment we felt from the dissipation of our dream of the fertile islands, I called this Disappointment Island.

"Out of the driftwood, we made ourselves pleasant little lodges, open to the water, and, after having kindled large fires to excite the wonder of any straggling savage on the lake shores, lay down, for the first time in a long journey, in perfect security; no one thinking about his arms. The evening was extremely bright and pleasant; but the wind rose during the night, and the waves began to break heavily on the shore, making our island tremble. I had not expected in our inland journey to hear the roar of an ocean surf; and the strangeness of our situation, and the excitement we felt in the associated interests of the place, made this one of the most interesting nights I remember during our long expedition.

"In the morning, the surf was breaking heavily on the shore, and we were up early. The lake was dark and agitated, and we hurried through our scanty breakfast, and embarked—having first filled one of the buckets with water from which it was intended to make salt. The sun had risen by the time we were ready to start; and it was blowing a strong gale of wind, almost directly off the shore, and raising a considerable sea, in which our boat strained very much. It roughened as we got away from the island, and it required all the efforts of the men to make any head against the wind and sea; the gale rising with the sun; and there was danger of being blown into one of the open reaches beyond the island. At the distance of half a mile from the beach, the depth of water was sixteen feet, with a clay bottom; but, as the working of the boat was very severe labor, and during the operation of sounding, it was necessary to cease paddling, during which the boat lost considerable way, I was unwilling to discourage the men, and reluctantly gave up my intention of ascertaining the depth and character of the bed. There was a general shout in the boat when we found ourselves in one fathom, and we soon after landed on a low point of mud, where we unloaded the boat, and carried the baggage to firmer ground."

CHAPTER XXIII.

THE RETURN—SUFFERING FOR FOOD—A ROYAL FEAST—ON THE LEWIS FORK—FORT HALL—DIVISION OF THE PARTY—ARRIVAL AT DALLES—THE SIERRA NEVADA—PREPARATIONS FOR THE PASSAGE THROUGH THE MOUNTAINS—FREMONT'S ACCOUNT.

The explorers remained in camp the next day and boiled down some of the water from the lake, thereby obtaining considerable salt. The following morning was clear and beautiful and they returned by the same route, ascending the valley of Bear River toward the north.

The expected Fitzpatrick and the provisions did not show themselves and the party began to suffer for food. When their situation became serious, Fremont permitted a horse to be killed and then all enjoyed one of their old fashioned feasts.

But this supply could not last long, and still they failed to meet their expected friends. After a time they encountered an Indian who had killed an antelope, which they quickly purchased and another feast made every heart glad. By way of dessert, a messenger galloped into camp with the news that Fitzpatrick was close at hand with an abundant supply of provisions.

The next morning the two parties united and continued the journey together. After leaving the Bear River Valley they crossed over to Lewis's Fork of the Columbia. At night the camp fires of the Indian twinkled like so many stars along the mountain side; but they were all friendly and the tired explorers slept peacefully.

Pushing onward they reached the upper waters of Lewis's Fork, where snow began to fall. However, they were quite near Fort Hall and they therefore went into camp, while Fremont rode to the fort and procured several horses and oxen.

The weather continued severe, but Fremont determined to push on, despite the hardships which he knew awaited them all. As a matter of prudence, however, he sent back eleven of his men, leaving about twenty with which he pursued his journey down the river valley in the direction of the Columbia. The Dalles was reached in safety where Kit Carson was left in command of the party, while Fremont with a few companions pushed on to Vancouver Island, where he procured some provisions. On his return, the whole party united and made their way to Klamath Lake, in what was then Oregon Territory. When their observations were completed, they took up their march in the direction of California.

After a long and wearisome journey, attended by much suffering for the lack of food, they came in sight of the Sierra Nevada Mountains, which were seen to be covered with snow. The men were in a sorry plight. The provisions were nearly gone; they could not turn back, and there seemed but two alternatives before them: to push on through the mountains or remain where they were and starve to death. Such men were not the ones to fold their hands and lie down in helpless despair. Accordingly, they made their preparations for the terrible venture.

The snow was so deep that it was impossible to get forward without the aid of snowshoes. Devoting themselves to the manufacture of these indispensable articles, a few were sent ahead to learn how far it was necessary to break a path for the animals. After a laborious passage, it was found that nine miles would have to be prepared in that fashion. Carson was with this advance and when they halted, he saw in the distance the green Sacramento Valley. Although nearly twenty years had passed since he visited that section, he recognized it at once. Away beyond towered the white peaks of the Coast Range. Carson was the only man in the party who really knew where they were.

This passage of Fremont and his men through the Sierra Nevada Mountains is one of the most extraordinary achievements in American history. Carson himself took such a prominent part in it, that it seems only just that Fremont's thrilling account should be quoted.

"The people were unusually silent; for every man knew that our enterprise was hazardous, and the issue doubtful.

"The snow deepened rapidly, and it soon became necessary to break a road. For this service, a party of ten was formed, mounted on the strongest horses; each man in succession opening the road on foot, or on horseback, until himself and his horse became fatigued, when he stepped aside; and, the remaining number passing ahead, he took his station in the rear.

"The camp had been all the day occupied in endeavoring to ascend the hill, but only the best horses had succeeded;

the animals, generally, not having sufficient strength to bring themselves up without the packs; and all the line of road between this and the springs was strewed with camp stores and equipage, and horses floundering in snow. I therefore immediately encamped on the ground with my own mess, which was in advance, and directed Mr. Fitzpatrick to encamp at the springs, and send all the animals, in charge of Tabeau, with a strong guard, back to the place where they had been pastured the night before. Here was a small spot of level ground, protected on one side by the mountain, and on the other sheltered by a little ridge of rock. It was an open grove of pines, which assimilated in size to the grandeur of the mountain, being frequently six feet in diameter.

"Tonight we had no shelter, but we made a large fire around the trunk of one of the huge pines; and covering the snow with small boughs, on which we spread our blankets, soon made ourselves comfortable. The night was very bright and clear, though the thermometer was only at 10 degrees. A strong wind which sprang up at sundown, made it intensely cold; and this was one of the bitterest nights during the journey.

"Two Indians joined our party here; and one of them, an old man, immediately began to harangue us, saying that ourselves and animals would perish in the snow; and that, if we would go back, he would show us another and a better way across the mountain. He spoke in a very loud voice, and there was a singular repetition of phrases and arrangement of words, which rendered his speech striking, and not unmusical.

"We had now begun to understand some words, and, with the aid of signs, easily comprehended the old man's simple ideas. 'Rock upon rock—rock upon rock—snow upon snow—snow upon snow,' said he; 'even if you get over the snow, you will not be able to get down from the mountains.' He made us the sign of precipices, and showed us how the feet of the horses would slip, and throw them off from the narrow trails led along their sides. Our Chinook, who comprehended even more readily than ourselves, and believed our situation hopeless, covered his head with his blanket, and began to weep and lament. 'I wanted to see the whites,' said he; 'I came away from my own people to see the whites, and I wouldn't care to die among them; but here'—and he looked around into the cold night and gloomy forest, and, drawing his blanket over his head, began again to lament.

"Seated around the tree, the fire illuminating the rocks and the tall boils of the pines round about, and the old Indian haranguing, we presented a group of very serious faces.

"February 5.—The night had been too cold to sleep, and we were up very early. Our guide was standing by the fire with all his finery on; and seeing him shiver in the cold, I threw on his shoulders one of my blankets. We missed him a few minutes afterwards, and never saw him again. He had deserted. His bad faith and treachery were in perfect keeping with the estimate of Indian character, which a long intercourse with this people had gradually forced upon my mind.

"While a portion of the camp were occupied in bringing up the baggage to this point, the remainder were busied in making sledges and snowshoes. I had determined to explore the mountain ahead, and the sledges were to be used in transporting the baggage.

"Crossing the open basin, in a march of about ten miles we reached the top of one of the peaks, to the left of the pass indicated by our guide. Far below us, dimmed by the distance, was a large, snowless valley, bounded on the western side, at the distance of about a hundred miles, by a low range of mountains, which Carson recognized with delight as the mountains bordering the coast. 'There,' said he, 'is the little mountain—it is fifteen years ago since I saw it; but I am just as sure as if I had seen it yesterday.' Between us, then, and this low coast range, was the valley of the Sacramento; and no one who had not accompanied us through the incidents of our life for the last few months, could realize the delight with which at last we looked down upon it. At the distance of apparently thirty miles beyond us were distinguished spots of prairie; and a dark line, which could be traced with the glass, was imagined to be the course of the river; but we were evidently at a great height above the valley, and between us and the plains extended miles of snowy fields and broken ridges of pine covered mountains.

"It was late in the day when we turned towards the camp; and it grew rapidly cold as it drew towards night. One of the men became fatigued and his feet began to freeze, and building a fire in the trunk of a dry old cedar, Mr. Fitzpatrick remained with him until his clothes could be dried, and he was in a condition to come on. After a day's march of twenty miles, we straggled into camp, one after another, at nightfall; the greater number excessively fatigued, only two of the party having ever travelled on snowshoes before.

"All our energies were now directed to getting our animals across the snow; and it was supposed that, after all the baggage had been drawn with the sleighs over the trail we had made, it would be sufficiently hard to bear our animals.

"At several places, between this point and the ridge, we had discovered some grassy spots, where the wind and sun had dispersed the snow from the sides of the hills, and these were to form resting place to support the animals for a night in their passage across. On our way across, we had set on fire several broken stumps and dried trees, to melt holes in the snow for the camp. Its general depth was five feet; but we passed over places where it was twenty feet deep, as shown by the trees.

"With one party drawing sleighs loaded with baggage, I advanced today about four miles along the trail, and encamped at the first grassy spot, where we expected to bring our horses. Mr. Fitzpatrick, with another party, remained behind, to form an intermediate station between us and the animals.

"Putting on our snowshoes, we spent the afternoon in exploring a road ahead. The glare of the snow, combined with great fatigue, had rendered many of the people nearly blind; but we were fortunate in having some black silk handkerchiefs, which, worn as veils, very much relieved the eye.

"In the evening I received a message from Mr. Fitzpatrick, acquainting me with the utter failure of his attempt to get our mules and horses over the snow—the half hidden trail had proved entirely too slight to support them, and they had broken through, and were plunging about or lying half buried in snow. He was occupied in endeavoring to get them back to his camp; and in the mean time sent to me for further instructions. I wrote to him to send the animals immediately back to their old pastures; and, after having made mauls and shovels, turn in all the strength of his party to open and beat a road through the snow, strengthening it with branches and boughs of the pines.

"February 12.—We made mauls, and worked hard at our end of the road all the day. The wind was high, but the sun bright, and the snow thawing. We worked down the face of the hill, to meet the people at the other end. Towards sundown it began to grow cold, and we shouldered our mauls, and trudged back to camp.

"February 13.—We continued to labor on the road; and in the course of the day had the satisfaction to see the people working down the face of the opposite hill, about three miles distant. During the morning we had the pleasure of a visit from Mr. Fitzpatrick, with the information that all was going on well. A party of Indians had passed on snowshoes, who said they were going to the western side of the mountain after fish. This was an indication that the salmon were coming up the streams; and we could hardly restrain our impatience as we thought of them, and worked with increased vigor.

"I was now perfectly satisfied that we had struck the stream on which Mr. Sutter lived, and turning about, made a hard push, and reached the camp at dark. Here we had the pleasure to find all the remaining animals, fifty-seven in number, safely arrived at the grassy hill near the camp; and here, also, we were agreeably surprised with the sight of an abundance of salt. Some of the horse guard had gone to a neighboring hut for pine nuts, and discovered unexpectedly a large cake of very white fine grained salt, which the Indians told them they had brought from the other side of the mountain; they used it to eat with their pine nuts, and readily sold it for goods.

"On the 19th, the people were occupied in making a road and bringing up the baggage; and, on the afternoon of the next day, February 20, 1844, we encamped with all the materiel of the camp, on the summit of the pass in the dividing ridge, 1,000 miles by our travelled road from the Dalles of the Columbia.

"February 21.—We now considered ourselves victorious over the mountain; having only the descent before us, and the valley under our eyes, we felt strong hope that we should force our way down. But this was a case in which the descent was not facile. Still, deep fields of snow lay between, and there was a large intervening space of rough looking mountains, through which we had yet to wind our way. Carson roused me this morning with an early fire, and we were all up long before day, in order to pass the snow fields before the sun should render the crust soft. We enjoyed this morning a scene at sunrise, which, even here, was unusually glorious and beautiful. Immediately above the eastern mountains was repeated a cloud formed mass of purple ranges, bordered with bright yellow gold; the peaks shot up into a narrow line of crimson cloud, above which the air was filled with a greenish orange; and over all was the singular beauty of the blue sky. Passing along a ridge which commanded the lake on our right, of which we began to discover an outlet through a chasm on the west, we passed over alternating open ground and hard crusted snow fields which supported the animals, and encamped on the ridge after a journey of six miles. The grass was better than we had yet seen, and we were encamped in a clump of trees, twenty or thirty feet high, resembling white pine."

CHAPTER XXIV.

CONTINUATION OF FREMONT'S ACCOUNT OF THE PASSAGE THROUGH THE MOUNTAINS.

"We had hard and doubtful labor yet before us, as the snow appeared to be heavier where the timber began further down, with few open spots. Ascending a height, we traced out the best line we could discover for the next day's march, and had at least the consolation to see that the mountain descended rapidly. The day had been one of April; gusty, with a few occasional flakes of snow; which, in the afternoon enveloped the upper mountains in clouds. We watched them anxiously, as now we dreaded a snow storm. Shortly afterwards we heard the roll of thunder, and looking toward the valley, found it all enveloped in a thunderstorm. For us, as connected with the idea of summer, it had a singular charm; and we watched its progress with excited feelings until nearly sunset, when the sky cleared off brightly, and we saw a shining line of water directing its course towards another, a broader and larger sheet. We knew that these could be no other than the Sacramento and the bay of San Francisco; but, after our long wandering in rugged mountains, where so frequently we had met with disappointments, and where the crossing of every ridge displayed some unknown lake or river, we were yet almost afraid to believe that we were at last to escape into the genial country of which we have heard so many glowing descriptions, and dreaded again to find some vast interior lake, whose bitter waters would bring us disappointment. On the southern shore of what appeared to be the bay, could be traced the gleaming line where entered another large stream; and again the Buenaventura rose up in our mind.

"Carson had entered the valley along the southern side of the bay, but the country then was so entirely covered with water from snow and rain, that he had been able to form no correct impression of watercourses.

"We had the satisfaction to know that at least there were people below. Fires were lit up in the valley just at night, appearing to be in answer to ours; and these signs of life renewed, in some measure, the gayety of the camp. They appeared so near, that we judged them to be among the timber of some of the neighboring ridges; but, having them constantly in view day after day, and night after night, we afterwards found them to be fires that had been kindled by the Indians among the tulares, on the shore of the bay, eighty miles distant.

"Axes and mauls were necessary today to make a road through the snow. Going ahead with Carson to reconnoitre the road, we reached in the afternoon the river which made the outlet of the lake. Carson sprang over, clear across a place where the stream was compressed among rocks, but the parfleche sole of my moccasin glanced from the icy rock, and precipitated me into the river. It was some few seconds before I could recover myself in the current, and Carson, thinking me hurt, jumped in after me, and we both had an icy bath. We tried to search a while for my gun, which had been lost in the fall, but the cold drove us out; and making a large fire on the bank, after we had partially dried ourselves we went back to meet the camp. We afterwards found that the gun had been slung under the ice which lined the banks of the creek.

"The sky was clear and pure, with a sharp wind from the northeast, and the thermometer 20 below the freezing point.

"We continued down the south face of the mountain; our road leading over dry ground, we were able to avoid the snow almost entirely. In the course of the morning we struck a foot path, which we were generally able to keep; and the ground was soft to our animals feet, being sandy or covered with mould. Green grass began to make its appearance, and occasionally we passed a hill scatteringly covered with it. The character of the forest continued the same; and, among the trees, the pine with sharp leaves and very large cones was abundant, some of them being noble trees. We measured one that had ten feet diameter, though the height was not more than one hundred and thirty feet. All along, the river was a roaring torrent, its fall very great; and, descending with a rapidity to which we had long been strangers, to our great pleasure oak trees appeared on the ridge, and soon became very frequent; on these I remarked unusually great quantities of mistletoe.

"The opposite mountain side was very steep and continuous— unbroken by ravines, and covered with pines and snow; while on the side we were travelling, innumerable rivulets poured down from the ridge. Continuing on, we halted a moment at one of these rivulets, to admire some beautiful evergreen trees, resembling live oak, which shaded the little stream. They were forty to fifty feet high, and two in diameter, with a uniform tufted top; and the summer green of their beautiful foliage, with the singing birds, and the sweet summer wind which was whirling about the dry oak leaves, nearly intoxicated us with delight; and we hurried on, filled with excitement, to escape entirely from the horrid region of inhospitable snow, to the perpetual spring of the Sacramento.

"February 25.—Believing that the difficulties of the road were passed, and leaving Mr. Fitzpatrick to follow slowly, as the condition of the animals required, I started ahead this morning with a party of eight, consisting (with myself) of Mr. Preuss, and Mr. Talbot, Carson, Derosier, Towns, Proue, and Jacob. We took with us some of the best animals, and my intention was to proceed as rapidly as possible to the house of Mr. Sutter, and return to meet the party with a supply of provisions and fresh animals.

"Near night fall we descended into the steep ravine of a handsome creek thirty feet wide, and I was engaged in getting the horses up the opposite hill, when I heard a shout from Carson, who had gone ahead a few hundred yards. 'Life yet,' said he, as he came up, 'life yet; I have found a hillside sprinkled with grass enough for the night.' We drove along our horses, and encamped at the place about dark, and there was just room enough to make a place for shelter on the edge of the stream. Three horses were lost today—Proveau; a fine young horse from the Columbia, belonging to Charles Towns; and another Indian horse which carried our cooking utensils; the two former gave out, and the latter strayed off into the woods as we reached the camp: and Derosier knowing my attachment to Proveau, volunteered to go and bring him in.

"Carson and I climbed one of the nearest mountains; the forest land still extended ahead, and the valley appeared as far as ever. The pack horse was found near the camp, but Derosier did not get in.

"We began to be uneasy at Derosier's absence, fearing he might have been bewildered in the woods. Charles Towns, who had not yet recovered his mind, went to swim in the river, as if it was summer, and the stream placid, when it was a cold mountain torrent foaming among the rocks. We were happy to see Derosier appear in the evening. He came in, and sitting down by the fire, began to tell us where he had been. He imagined he had been gone several days, and thought we were still at the camp where he had left us; and we were pained to see that his mind was deranged. It appeared that he had been lost in the mountain, and hunger and fatigue, joined to weakness of body, and fear of perishing in the mountains had crazed him. The times were severe when stout men lost their minds from extremity of suffering—when horses died—and when mules and horses, ready to die of starvation, were killed for food. Yet there was no murmuring or hesitation. In the meantime Mr. Preuss continued on down the river, and unaware that we had encamped so early in the day, was lost. When night arrived and he did not come in, we began to understand what had happened to him; but it was too late to make any search.

"March 3.—We followed Mr. Preuss's trail for a considerable distance along the river, until we reached a place where he had descended to the stream below and encamped. Here we shouted and fired guns, but received no answer; and we concluded that he had pushed on down the stream. I determined to keep out from the river, along which it was nearly impracticable to travel with animals, until it should form a valley. At every step the country improved in beauty; the pines were rapidly disappearing, and oaks became the principal trees of the forest. Among these, the prevailing tree was the evergreen oak (which, by way of distinction, we shall call the live oak); and with these, occurred frequently a new species of oak, bearing a long, slender acorn, from an inch to an inch and a half in length, which we now began to see formed the principal vegetable food of the inhabitants of this region. In a short distance we crossed a little rivulet, where were two old huts and near by were heaps of acorn hulls. The ground round about was very rich, covered with an exuberant sward of grass; and we sat down for a while in the shade of the oaks to let the animals feed. We repeated our shouts for Mr. Preuss; and this time we were gratified with an answer. The voice grew rapidly nearer, ascending from the river, but when we expected to see him emerge, it ceased entirely. We had called up some straggling Indian—the first we had met, although for two days back we had seen tracks—who, mistaking us for his fellows, had been only undeceived by getting close up. It would have been pleasant to witness his astonishment; he would not have been more frightened had some of the old mountain spirits they are so much afraid of suddenly appeared in his path. Ignorant of the character of these people, we had now additional cause of uneasiness in regard to Mr. Preuss; he had no arms with him, and we began to think his chance doubtful. Occasionally we met deer, but had not the necessary time for hunting. At one of these orchard grounds, we encamped about noon to make an effort for Mr. Preuss. One man took his way along a spur leading into the river, in hope to cross his trail, and another took our own back. Both were volunteers; and to the successful man was promised a pair of pistols—not as a reward, but as a token of gratitude for a service which would free us all from much anxiety."

At the end of four days, Mr. Preuss surprised and delighted his friends by walking into camp. He had lived on roots and acorns and was in the last stages of exhaustion.

Shortly the advance party reached Sutter's Fort where they received the most hospitable treatment. All their wants were abundantly supplied, and provisions were sent back to Fitzpatrick and his party.

CHAPTER XXV.

THE START HOMEWARD—THE VISITORS IN CAMP AND THEIR STORY—CARSON AND GODEY START TO THE RESCUE—TRAILING THE ENEMY BY NIGHT—IN CAMP—THE ATTACK—AN AMAZING SUCCESS—THE RETURN.

Fremont and his command remained at Sutter's Fort about a month, when their preparations were completed for their return to the States. They journeyed leisurely up the valley of the San Joaquin, crossing over the Sierra Nevada and Coast Range by means of an easily travelled pass. The latter chain was followed until they came upon the Spanish trail, along which they passed to the Mohave River. Where the Trail diverges from that stream, Carson became involved in a characteristic adventure.

While in camp two Mexicans, a man and a boy, rode up and told a sad story. They belonged to a party of Mexican traders from New Mexico. Six of them, including two women who acted as cooks, were left in charge of a band of horses while the rest were away, engaged in barter. When endeavoring to find better grazing for their animals and while the man and boy were on guard, they were attacked by a band of thirty Indians.

The warriors were after the horses and their first demonstration was a flight of arrows. The only chance of escape was to make off with the animals and the two started them on a dead run straight toward the Indians. The charge was so impetuous, that they forced their way through, and continued their flight, while the warriors remained behind to massacre the others.

When the couple had gone a long distance, they left the horses and turned back to look for their friends. While they were doing so, they came upon Fremont's camp. When it is added that among those who were left behind by the Mexicans, were the wife of the man and the father and mother of the boy, their pitiful situation must touch the hearts of all. They were overcome with grief, and Carson was so stirred that he volunteered to go back with the couple and help rescue their friends if alive, or punish the Indians, if it should prove that they had been massacred.

Richard Godey, a mountaineer almost the equal with Carson, willingly agreed to accompany him. The two were perfectly familiar with the country, which was an immense advantage. When the Mexicans described the spring, a long ways distant, where they had abandoned the horses to hunt for their friends, Carson recalled its exact location. It was about thirty miles away and he said that that was the point toward which they must push with all speed.

Accordingly they turned the heads of their horses thither and struck into a sweeping gallop, resting only when compelled to do so, and reaching the spring at daylight the next morning. Not a horse was visible, but an examination of the ground showed that the Indians had followed the fleeing Mexicans and stock to the spring, where, finding the animals, they had captured and driven them off in another direction.

It seems like a piece of madness for three men to pursue ten times as many Indian warriors; but the blood of Carson was up and he told Godey it was too soon for them to turn back. The eyes of both flashed, when they reflected upon the shameful outrage, and they meant that the marauders should not get off scot free.

As the boy was only an incumbrance, he was left behind, and, taking the trail of the warriors, the three put their horses to their best, confident the chase would be a long one. On such occasions, the red men are accustomed to travel a long distance before making a halt. With so much booty in their hands, they were liable to be set upon by others as savage as themselves, and they had every cause, therefore, to get out of the country with the least possible delay.

The three were riding in this furious fashion, when most unexpectedly the steed of the Mexican gave out. A minute's examination showed he was as thoroughly used up and useless as the horse of the Ute Indian, years before, who started out with Kit to pursue the thief that was running off with the animals. There was no course but to leave the Mexican behind, for time was too precious to ride back to camp after another horse. He, therefore was told to go back to Fremont's camp and await their return.

The exploit of Carson and Godey, when calmly told, seems incredible. There was no one in Fremont's command who would go with them, and though they knew there were a score and a half of savage wild men to encounter, they did not hesitate, but pressed their steeds to the utmost, eager to join in the fierce hand to hand conflict.

When night shut in upon them, the Indians were not in sight and the signs indicated they were a good many miles ahead. There was no moon or stars and they could see only a few feet in advance of their horses' ears, but it would not do to linger. If they should go into camp, they would lose so much ground that pursuit was likely to be hopeless.

Accordingly, they dismounted and leading their steeds, continued the pursuit on foot. Where it was impossible to see the ground, they depended on the sense of feeling. Quite certain of the general direction taken by the red men, they occasionally stooped down and passed their hands over the earth. The trail was so distinct that it could be readily detected in this manner, provided they had not gone astray. Several times they wandered to the right or left, but found their way back without difficulty, and the chase was continued for several hours in this singular fashion.

After a time, the trail became so fresh that it could be readily detected and no doubt was left in their minds that they were close upon the marauders. Inasmuch as Carson and Godey had pushed their horses to the utmost, and they were showing signs of weariness, they concluded, in view of these facts, to halt and wait until daylight.

The night was unusually cold, but they dared not start a fire, lest it should apprise their enemies of their presence. So they suffered in silence, miserable, wretched and as uncomfortable as it was possible to be, while watching for the growing light in the east.

When at last, morning appeared, they were so chilled that they could hardly walk; but making their way to the bottom of a ravine, they kindled a fire, and with the help of some violent exercise, managed to start their blood in circulation.

In a very brief time, their horses were resaddled and they were galloping along the trail again. Within an hour, they caught sight of the Indians and the stolen animals. The warriors were in camp and were enjoying a breakfast of horse meat, several of the stock having been killed to furnish the food.

Before the Indians could detect their pursuers, the latter dismounted and hid their steeds where they were not likely to attract notice. They then started to crawl in among the stolen animals, which were grazing a short distance from camp. This was an exceedingly delicate task, for the horses were likely to give the alarm, even if the warriors did not detect their presence; but patience and skill succeeded, and, after a time, they were among the drove.

But the very thing they dreaded took place. They had scarcely reached the animals, when one of them became frightened by the appearance of the strangers, and began rearing and snorting. This caused such confusion among the others that the Indians became alarmed and sprang to their feet. Carson and Godey emitted a series of yells that must have made the red men envious, and dashed at full speed toward the thirty Indians. The moment they were within range, both fired. Carson killed his man, but Godey missed. The latter reloaded with great quickness and fired again, bringing down his man.

Meanwhile, the warriors were thrown into a sort of panic by the amazing audacity of their assailants. They could not have suspected the truth—that is that no others were near. They must have believed that a strong reserve was close at hand and that if they tarried in camp they would be overwhelmed by a party of avengers. Accordingly they broke and ran, leaving the daring mountaineers masters of the field.

In accordance with the savage spirit of the border, Godey scalped the two Indians who had been shot, after which the horses were gathered together and driven to where the steeds of the mountaineers had been left.

But when this point was reached, Carson expressed himself as not satisfied: they had not ascertained the fate of the captives and they now proceeded to do so.

In the camp of the Mexicans were found the mangled bodies of the two men. These were buried by Carson and Godey who made search for the women. Though nothing of them was discovered, it was afterwards learned that they, too, had been killed. Having done all that was possible, Carson and Godey made their way back to Fremont's camp, where the stolen property was turned over to the Mexicans, the daring mountaineers refusing to accept the slightest payment for their extraordinary services.

CHAPTER XXVI.

ARRIVAL AT BENT'S FORT—CARSON GOES TO TAOS AND DECIDES TO BECOME A FARMER—ARRIVAL OF A MESSENGER FROM FREMONT—CARSON AND OWENS REPAIR AGAIN TO BENT'S FORT—CARSON ENGAGES AS GUIDE FOR FREMONT'S THIRD EXPLORING EXPEDITION—ON THE GREAT DIVIDE—DIVISION OF THE PARTIES—THE JOURNEY ACROSS THE DESERT—A SINGULAR MEETING—ABORIGINAL HORSE THIEVES.

After a tedious journey of many miles, the exploring party reached Bent's Fort July 2, 1844. The labors were considered finished, and bidding his old commander goodbye, Carson made his way to Taos, where he had a most happy reunion with his family. He was cordially welcomed by hundreds of old friends who had learned years before the rare courage and worth of the man, and who were proud to possess such a neighbor.

Carson had led a wild and adventurous career, and, after talking much with those in whom he had confidence, he decided to adopt the life of a farmer. In this conclusion he was joined by Richard Owens, an old mountaineer and an intimate associate for many years.

It did not take them long to fix upon a desirable site, and, in the spring of 1845, stock and animals were bought, building commenced and everything was fairly under way. At the moment when the scarred mountaineers were counting with pleasure on the complete arrangements made, an express messenger galloped up and handed Carson a letter.

The contents were of an important character. Captain Fremont had written to notify Kit that he had started on his third exploring expedition, and, inasmuch as the mountaineer had given his promise months before, that in the event of doing so, he (Carson) would serve again as guide, Fremont reminded him that he should hold him to his pledge and would expect to meet him at Bent's Fort on his arrival there.

It was a considerable pecuniary sacrifice for Carson to keep his promise, but he never failed to do so, when it was not absolutely impossible. Besides, it is fair to presume that the old life could never lose its charm for one of his disposition, and, contrasted with the humdrum existence of a farmer, he could not have been much grieved over the reception of the message. But it must be stated that both Owens and Carson sold out at much loss, and, putting their affairs in the best shape possible, bade families and friends goodbye, mounted their horses and set out for Bent's Fort which was safely reached some days later.

There they were warmly welcomed by Fremont, who had entered upon his third exploring expedition, the last under the authority of the United States government, though two others were afterwards undertaken on his own responsibility. As was to be supposed, Fremont taking lessons from his previous experiences, was much better equipped for his third than for either of the other preceding expeditions. He had about fifty men, among them in addition to Carson and Owens, being Maxwell, the famous mountaineer, Walker who was a member of Captain Bonneville's expedition to the Columbia, besides other hunters and scouts less known but not less skilful and daring than they.

We have already given tolerably full accounts of the two exploring expeditions of Fremont, and it is not our purpose to narrate the particulars of the one which followed. There is a sameness in many of the occurrences but the third time the Pathfinder penetrated into the recesses of the far west, he became involved in a series of experiences totally different from the preceding and deeply interesting of themselves.

Several months were spent on what may be called the Great Divide—that is the region where the waters flow east or west to either ocean, and in the autumn of the year they encamped on the southwestern shore of the Great Salt Lake.

Before them stretched a vast arid plain to which the trappers referred with a shudder of terror. They had heard of it many a time and the common legend was that no man white or Indian who had ever attempted to cross it, succeeded. These stories, however, added to the eagerness of Captain Fremont to explore its secrets, and, when he proposed it to his men, they expressed as strong a desire as he to do so. They felt a mutual trust and confidence impossible under other circumstances.

Some seventy miles away, a mountain peak held out the promise of wood and water. Four men under the guidance of an Indian, were sent forward to explore the place, and, in the event of finding water, they were instructed to apprise the watchful commander by means of the smoke from a camp fire.

When the second day closed without sight of the signal,

Fremont became so uneasy that he moved forward with the rest of the party and travelled all night. At daylight, one of the smaller party approached them. He said that running water and grass existed at the mountains, but their Indian guide was wholly ignorant of the country. This was good news and the next day the party reached the stream.

Shortly after, the expedition was divided into two parties, Walker (of whom mention has been made), taking charge of the larger while Fremont led the smaller. It was the purpose of Walker to pass around to the foot of the Sierra Nevada, by a route with which he was familiar, while Fremont with Carson and less than a dozen men, among whom were several Delaware Indians, headed straight across the desert.

While advancing over this arid tract, they detected a volume of smoke rising from a ravine. Cautiously approaching, they discovered an Indian warrior perfectly nude, standing by a fire and watching an earthen pot in which something was simmering. He was greatly frightened and offered them his food. They smiled, treated him kindly and gave him several trifling presents which he received with childish delight.

One of the singular incidents of the journey took place while the exploring party were making their way along the foot of the Sierras. Passing around a point on the lake shore, they unexpectedly met a dozen Indian warriors. They were walking directly behind each other in what is known as Indian file, their heads bent forward and their eyes fixed on the ground. The whites turned aside to allow them to pass and naturally watched them with much interest. The Indians neither halted, deviated from the path, spoke nor looked up, but walked straight forward with their silent, measured tread until they disappeared. The explorers did not interfere with them or speak to them. Thus the representatives of the different races encountered.

The division under charge of Walker joined Fremont at the appointed rendezvous, but winter was upon them, the mountains were sure to be choked with snow and no one was familiar with the route. As a matter of prudence, therefore, Walker was directed to continue southward with the principal party, while Fremont and a few picked men pushed on directly through the Sierras to Sutter's Fort, with a view of obtaining the necessary animals and supplies.

The smaller division was advancing as best it could, when a number of plainly marked trails were observed showing they were in the vicinity of some of the most notorious horse thieves in the world. They were daring and skilful, went long distances, plundered ranches and hastened to the mountains with their booty. The exasperated Californians often organized and went in pursuit, but it was rare they overtook the dusky thieves, and when they succeeded in doing so, were invariably defeated.

This sort of people were undesirable neighbors, and Fremont sent forward two Delawares and two mountaineers to make an investigation. They had not gone far, when the company following them found the signs so threatening that they were alarmed for the scouts. A short distance further they came upon such an excellent camping site that they decided to halt for the night.

CHAPTER XXVII.

ALARMING SOUNDS—DANGER OF THE SCOUTS—
FREMONT GOES TO THEIR RESCUE—ARRIVAL AT
SUTTER'S FORT—ORDERED OUT OF CALIFORNIA BY
THE MEXICAN GOVERNOR—FREMONT'S REFUSAL—
WITHDRAWAL TO SACRAMENTO RIVER—ARRIVAL
OF DESPATCHES FROM WASHINGTON—WAR WITH
MEXICO—MEETING WITH LIEUTENANT GILLESPIE—
NIGHT ATTACK BY KLAMATH INDIANS.

While preparing to go into camp, the explorers were mystified by hearing a number of peculiar sounds like the barking of dogs. Attentive listening, however, satisfied them that it came from an Indian village close by, whose women and children were calling out and lamenting. This constituted positive proof that the friends in advance were in trouble with the red men and there was not a minute to lose in going to their rescue.

A half mile further, the explorers galloped over a slight ridge, when they suddenly came in sight of several hundred Indians, who were making their way up two sides of a knoll, on the crest of which the four scouts had entrenched themselves among the rocks and trees and were coolly awaiting the attack of their enemies.

The little party had run so suddenly into danger that they were compelled to make a flying leap from their horses, in order to secure a suitable shelter. The assailants had almost captured the abandoned horses, when relief came. The two Delawares made a dash to recover their animals, their companions shooting the foremost of the thieves. The property was saved and then all fell back to their own camp.

As the aboriginal horse thieves were so numerous, Fremont kept up an unremitting watch all through the night. Singular noises were continually heard and there could be no doubt that the women and children were retreating further into the mountains.

One of the Delawares on guard was sure he saw an Indian leap over a log, and firing quickly, brought him to the ground; but it proved to be a prowling wolf. None of their enemies appeared, and when morning came, Fremont withdrew from his perilous position.

Sutter's Fort at last was safely reached, and the other party having become lost, Carson was sent to find them. He succeeded with little difficulty and the companies reunited.

Their course was now directed toward Monterey on the sea coast, where they were confident of securing all they needed, but before reaching the place, a messenger arrived from General Castro, the Mexican commander of the territory, ordering the Americans to leave at once or they would be driven out.

Fremont immediately intrenched himself and waited for the Mexicans to carry out their threat. He waited three days, and then, as no attempt was made, withdrew to the Sacramento, which stream was followed to Lawson's Trading Post, where the commander hoped to purchase the outfit for the journey homeward.

Moving northward toward the Columbia, they encountered an enormous force of marauding Indians with whom a fierce battle was fought. The savages were defeated and lost a large number of warriors.

While encamped near Klamath Lake, two horsemen galloped up with despatches to Fremont from Washington, forwarded by Lieutenant Gillespie, of the United States Marines. This officer was making his way through the Indian country with six men as an escort, when his animals began to succumb. Fearing he would not be able to intercept the Captain, the Lieutenant selected two of his best men and sent them ahead with the despatches. He begged Fremont to forward him assistance, as he doubted his ability to reach him without such help.

But the most startling news brought to camp was that war had been declared between the United States and Mexico. When Fremont had read his despatches from his Government, he appreciated the imminent danger in which the Lieutenant was placed, and, without any tarrying, perfected measures for his rescue.

He immediately selected ten of his men, Carson, as a matter of course being among them, and pushed on with all haste, leaving directions for the rest to follow as rapidly as they could.

Fremont and his little company had journeyed something over fifty miles when they met the officer and his companions. The meeting was of the happiest nature, for the Lieutenant, in fact, was in greater danger than he suspected, the Indians around him being among the most treacherous of their race.

Those who have been placed in a situation resembling in a

slight degree that of Fremont, can appreciate the interest with which he perused the letters and papers from his distant home. After the parties had gone into camp, the Captain sat up till after midnight reading by the light of the camp fire. Tired out at last, he stretched out with his blanket about him and sank soon into heavy slumber.

The night was cold, and Carson and Owens, with their saddle blankets wrapped around them, lay down close to the fire. All at once Carson heard a peculiar noise, as though some one had struck a quick blow with an axe. Wondering what it could mean, he called to one of the mountaineers.

"What's the matter over there?"

There was no answer, for the head of the poor fellow had been cleft by an axe in the hands of one of the Klamath Indians who had crept into camp. A Delaware had already been killed by the treacherous redskins, that night being the second among all those spent in the west, when the explorers had no sentinel on duty.

Carson and Owens called out "Indians!" and springing to their feet, hurried away from the fire whose strong light was sure to tempt the aim of their enemies.

One of the other Delawares who leaped to his feet snatched up the nearest rifle which unfortunately was not his own, and was unloaded. Unaware of the fact, he tried to fire it over again and again, without suspecting the cause, while a Klamath launched arrow after arrow into his body. The first penetrated his left breast and was fatal; but he bravely kept his feet trying to discharge the useless gun, until four other missiles were also buried within a few inches of the first.

Kit Carson had been quick to detect the danger of the brave

Delaware, and, in the hope of saving his life, he brought his unerring rifle to his shoulder. Just as his finger pressed the trigger, he recollected that that, too, was unloaded.

By one of those singular fatalities which sometimes occur, Carson had broken the tube the night before, and left the weapon unloaded. Without trifling with it, he threw it down, drew his single barrelled pistol and ran toward the Klamath, who was coolly launching his arrows into the breast of the poor Delaware.

The Indian leaped from side to side, so as to distract the aim of his enemies, and, instead of hitting him, Carson only cut the string which held a tomahawk to the warrior's arm. The mountaineer had no other shot at command, and Maxwell tried his hand, but in the uncertain light, inflicted only a slight wound. The Indian at that moment wheeled to run, when one of the whites shot him dead. By this time the alarm was general and the assailants fled.

There was good reason to believe that the Klamath Indians had set the snare for Lieutenant Gillespie and his escort. As it was, the wonder was that Fremont's command did not suffer to a greater extent; for having no sentinels on duty, the warriors might have perfected their schemes in security and killed a large number.

The Indian who drove five arrows into the left breast of the Delaware, three of which pierced his heart, was the leader of the attacking party. He had an English half axe slung to his wrist by a cord, and forty arrows were left in his quiver. Carson pronounced them the most beautiful and warlike missiles he had ever seen.

As may be supposed the explorers "slept on their arms" for

the rest of the night, but the assailants had fled.

They had killed three of the explorers, besides wounding another of the Delawares, who took characteristic revenge by scalping the leader that had been left where he fell. The dead were given the best burial possible. As illustrating the ingratitude and perfidy of these red men, it may be stated that it was only a few days before that they had visited Fremont's camp, and, though provisions were very scarce, they had been given considerable food, besides tobacco and a number of presents.

CHAPTER XXVIII.

RETALIATORY MEASURES—FREMONT'S RETURN TO CALIFORNIA—CAPTURE OF SONOMA—SUTTER'S FORT PLACED UNDER MILITARY RULE—MONTEREY TAKEN BY COMMODORE SLOAT—CAPTURE OF LOS ANGELES BY FREMONT AND COMMODORE STOCKTON—CARSON SENT EAST AS A BEARER OF DESPATCHES—THE MEETING WITH APACHES—GENERAL KEARNEY—BRAVERY OF THE CALIFORNIA MEXICANS.

The indignation over the action of the Indians was so great that retaliatory measures were determined upon. Fremont moved around Lake Klamath until nearly opposite where his command had been attacked. The following morning, Carson and ten men were sent forward to search for the Indian village that was believed to be somewhere in the neighborhood. If the discovery could be made without detection on the part of the Indians, Carson was instructed to signal to Fremont who would hasten forward with reinforcements.

The mountaineer had not gone far, when he struck a broad, clear trail, which speedily carried him in sight of a village of some fifty lodges. As it was evident that the Indians had detected their danger, Carson and his companions made an impetuous attack before which the red men fled in wildest panic. A number were shot, when, finding pursuit useless, Carson returned to the village where all the lodges were destroyed.

Because of the war with Mexico, Fremont decided to return to California. On his way thither, the Tlamath Indians continually dogged them and a number of collisions followed, though none was of particular moment. After suffering many hardships, Lawson's Fort was reached and several days were spent in hunting, while Fremont awaited instructions as to the course he was to take in the war then going on between the United States and Mexico.

As the days went by without bringing him any despatches, he wearied of inactivity and decided to assume the aggressive. Accordingly he sent a force to a Mexican military post known as Sonoma, which with little trouble was taken.

Fremont sent out a couple of messengers to inform the American settlers of what had taken place, but the messengers fell into the hands of General Castro who put both to death.

General Castro sent one of his captains, with quite a force to destroy the Americans, but the officer changed his mind when he found himself in the neighborhood of the detested invaders. Fremont pursued him for nearly a week, and captured much of his stock and property, but the Mexican was so skilful in retreating that he could not be brought to bay and Fremont returned to Sonoma.

The little force under Fremont now became the rallying point for the American settlers, and before long the Captain had several hundred under his command. Leaving a garrison at

Sonoma, he marched to Sutter's Fort, which was placed under military rule, and then made his way toward Monterey with the purpose of capturing that town. On his arrival, however, he found the place had already been taken by Commodore Sloat and the American squadron. The Commodore leaving shortly after, Commodore Stockton succeeded him.

While at Sonoma, Fremont and his comrades had declared the independence of California and adopted the Bear Flag, which was proffered to Commodore Sloat and the Star Spangled Banner hoisted over the camp.

As the Mexican General, Castro, was known to be at Los Angeles, Fremont asked for and obtained a ship on which his force was taken to San Diego. Then with a much inferior force, he set out to give battle to the Mexican leader; but the latter no sooner learned of his coming, than he fled with all his men. Finding it impossible to force him to give battle, Fremont encamped near the town, where he waited until joined by Commodore Stockton and a company of marines.

The junction effected, they marched upon Los Angeles which immediately fell into their hands. Long before this, Fremont had become impressed with the necessity of having some communication with Washington. In one sense it may be said he was all at sea, for he was without positive instructions, at a critical period, when it was most important that his line of policy should be clearly defined by his government.

But the matter of communicating with headquarters, thousands of miles away, was infinitely more difficult and serious than it is today. A vast, wild, perilous and almost unknown tract stretched between the Pacific and Atlantic, across which it required weeks and sometimes months for an express rider to make his way. To send despatches around Cape Horn took a much longer time; but the necessity was so urgent that Fremont sent Carson with fifteen picked men across the plains, instructing him to complete the journey if possible in sixty days.

Carson started in the middle of September, 1846, and by the exercise of his consummate skill he passed rapidly through a most dangerous section without running into any special danger until the third day. Then, when in the neighborhood of the copper mines of New Mexico, he suddenly came upon an encampment of Apaches, one of the most hostile tribes and the most daring of fighters in the whole southwest.

This was another of those critical occasions where Carson's wonderful quickness of mind enabled him to make the right decision without a second's delay. He understood the language, customs and peculiarities of the people, and he knew them to be splendid riders and tiger-like warriors. The least evidence of timidity would invite an overwhelming attack: a bold front and what may be called indomitable "cheek" were all that was likely to take them through.

Telling his men to halt, Carson galloped forward until within a few rods of the warriors, when he reined up and called out that he wished to hold a parley with them. Thereupon, a number advanced to hear what he had to say. The mountaineer stated that he and his friends were simply travellers through the Apache country; while they were prepared for war, they desired peace, and as their animals were tired out they wished to exchange them for fresh ones. The Apaches expressed themselves satisfied with the proposal, and Carson carefully chose a camping site, where they could best protect themselves against treachery. Then the exchange was made, both parties being so well satisfied that they parted with many expressions of good will.

It was impossible to carry any extended stock of provisions, the party depending upon their rifles to supply their needs in that direction; but game proved to be very scarce and they suffered much until they reached the first Mexican settlement. Although those people were at war with the United States, their friendship for Carson led them to supply abundantly all the wants of himself and friends.

With unremitting diligence and skill, the party pushed on day after day until the sixth of October, when, as they were riding across a treeless prairie, several moving specks were observed in the far horizon. As they came closer, they resolved themselves into horsemen, and, with a delight which may be imagined, Carson speedily observed that they were a detachment of United States troops under the command of General S. W. Kearney, who was highly pleased to meet Carson.

The detachment was a strong one and was on its way to operate in California. After that officer had obtained all the important news Carson had to give, he decided to send the despatches to Washington by another, while he employed the mountaineer to guide him back.

This delicate duty was executed with such admirable skill that General Kearney commended Carson in the highest terms. So rapidly did they move that California was entered early in December, and they were approaching San Diego, when the scouts brought news that a large party of Mexicans were intrenched a short distance ahead with the intention of disputing their advance. Fifteen men under Carson were sent forward to drive in the outposts and capture such loose animals as could be found.

A fierce fight followed, the Mexicans showing far more daring and skill than was expected. General Kearney was compelled to send two companies of dragoons and twenty-five California volunteers to charge the enemy. Carson was in the front column, and was riding at high speed, when his horse stumbled, throwing him so violently as to shatter the stock of his gun. He lay partly stunned but speedily recovering, he caught up the rifle of a dead dragoon and rushed into the fight. Though the Mexicans were finally driven out, they inflicted frightful loss on the Americans. Nearly every man who was in the front column, where Carson was riding when his horse threw him, was killed by the deadly bullets of the enemy.

The Mexicans soon rallied and attacked the Americans with such fierceness that the advance guard was driven back and forced to act on the defensive. No soldiers could have fought with greater gallantry than did the assailants. Before the two mountain howitzers could be unlimbered, almost every man around them was shot down. Then the Mexicans charged forward, lassoed the horses, captured one of the guns and turned it on the Americans. From some cause or other it could not be discharged. Finally, the Americans took refuge among the rocks, where they were surrounded by three or four times their number, seemingly with the choice of two courses before them—to surrender or starve to death.

CHAPTER XXIX.

DARING EXPLOIT OF KIT CARSON AND LIEUTENANT BEALE—GENERAL KEARNEY SAVED.

The situation of General Kearney and his men could not have been more desperate. The only subsistence they had were their mules, and the water was insufficient to meet their wants. They were completely surrounded by the brave California Mexicans. They might exist for a time on the bodies of their animals, but they must perish without water.

General Kearney called his friends together during the afternoon to consult as to whether any possible means of escape was before them. He could see none. He had sent three scouts to Commodore Stockton at San Diego, asking for immediate help, but the three were captured by the Mexicans on their return. Kearney had succeeded in exchanging a Mexican lieutenant, whom he held prisoner, for one of the scouts, but nothing was gained thereby. The messenger reported that they had been unable to reach San Diego, and Commodore Stockton, therefore, was in ignorance of the peril of his countrymen not far distant.

When every one expressed himself as unable to see the first ray of hope, Carson in his deliberate, modest way said that it was clear only a single possibility remained—that was by procuring relief from Commodore Stockton at San Diego. Though the other scouts had failed to reach him, Carson expressed his belief that he could succeed. At any rate, he desired to make the attempt to pass the Mexican lines.

Lieutenant Beale, since Minister to Austria, and favorably known throughout the country, immediately seconded the proposition, volunteering to accompany Carson. General Kearney gladly and gratefully accepted the offer, and the arrangements were instantly made. These arrangements were of the simplest nature. The beleaguered Americans were surrounded by three cordons of sentinels, and it was necessary for Carson and Beale to make their way past them in order to reach San Diego.

When night was fully descended, the two left the rocks and approaching the first line, sank upon their hands and knees, and crawled forward with the silence and stealth of Indian scouts. Despite the utmost care, their shoes made a slight noise now and then, and to avoid it, they took them off and shoved them in their belts.

The exploit of Lieutenant Beale and Kit Carson was a most remarkable one in every respect. Frequently through the gloom they would catch the faint outlines of a sentinel, pacing back and forth. Instantly the two would lie flat on their faces until the man moved away, when the painful progress would be resumed.

The slightest forgetfulness was certain to prove fatal, for the Mexicans, knowing the desperate straits of the Americans, must have been expecting some such attempt and were therefore more than usually watchful.

Once a mounted Mexican rode close to the prostrate figures, sprang off his horse and lit his cigarette. He was so close that the tiny flame showed his nose and features, as it was held in front of his face, while lighting the twist of tobacco. During that most trying moment, as Kit Carson afterwards declared, he distinctly heard the beating of Lieutenant Beale's heart.

There seemed no escape but finally the horseman drove away and the painful progress was continued for fully two miles, during which both men were constantly peering through the darkness for signs of danger. Again and again they were compelled to halt, and lying flat on their faces, wait till their fate was determined.

"We are through," whispered Carson at last, when considerable distance beyond the last row of sentinels.

"Thank heaven!" exclaimed Lieutenant Beale in the same guarded voice.

"Now we'll put on our shoes and travel as fast as we know how to San Diego—"

The mountaineer paused in dismay, for, while creeping over the plain, he had lost both his shoes that were thrust in his belt. The Lieutenant had been equally unfortunate, and, as it was utterly out of their power to recover them, they could only push on barefooted, over a soil that abounded with thorns and prickly pears. As these could not be seen in the darkness, their feet were soon wounded to a distressing degree. It was necessary to avoid the well beaten trails, so that the route was not only made longer, but much more difficult on account of the obstacles named.

Yet they were working for a great stake. The lives of General Kearney and his brave men were in the balance. If Carson and

Beale failed to bring help right speedily, they were doomed.

All night long, through the succeeding day and far into the following night, the couple, worn, wearied and with bleeding feet, pushed ahead. When exhausted, they would halt for a brief while, but the thought of their imperilled comrades, and the fear that some of the Mexicans were pursuing them, speedily started them off again and they kept to their work with a grim resolution which heeded not fatigue, suffering and wounds.

The only compass Carson had was his eye, but he was so familiar with the country that he never lost himself. The weary men were still trudging forward, when through the darkness ahead suddenly flashed out a star-like point of light. Several others appeared and a minute after they dotted the background of gloom like a constellation.

"That's San Diego!" exclaimed Carson, who could not be mistaken. The couple could scarcely restrain their joy. New life and activity thrilled their bodies, and they hurried on with the same elastic eagerness they felt at the beginning.

In a short while they were challenged by sentinels, and making known their mission, were taken before Commodore Stockton. That officer, with his usual promptness, sent a force of nearly two hundred men to the relief of General Kearney. They took with them a piece of ordnance which for want of horses the men themselves were forced to draw.

They advanced by forced marches to the endangered Americans, scarcely pausing night or day, until in sight of the Mexicans, who considering discretion the better part of valor, withdrew without exchanging a shot with the naval brigade.

As may be supposed, the feet of Carson and Beale were in a frightful condition, when they reached San Diego.

The mountaineer, on that account, did not return with the reinforcements, but he described the course and location so minutely that no difficulty was experienced by the relieving force.

Lieutenant Beale was a man of sturdy frame, accustomed to roughing it on the frontier, but the sufferings he underwent on that eventful night were such that he felt the effects for years afterward.

CHAPTER XXX.

CAPTURE OF LOS ANGELES—COURT MARTIAL OF FREMONT—CARSON APPOINTED A BEARER OF DISPATCHES TO WASHINGTON—HIS JOURNEY TO ST. LOUIS—VISITS WASHINGTON—APPOINTED LIEUTENANT BY PRESIDENT POLK—ORDERED BACK ACROSS THE CONTINENT—HIS JOURNEY—ASSIGNED TO DUTY AT TAJON PASS—AGAIN ORDERED TO WASHINGTON—HIS APPOINTMENT NOT CONFIRMED BY THE UNITED STATES SENATE—VISIT TO WASHINGTON—RETURN TO NEW MEXICO.

The chief force of the Mexicans was at Los Angeles over a hundred miles to the north of San Diego. They numbered six or seven hundred and were strongly intrenched. General Kearney and Commodore Stockton joined their commands and marched to attack them. Arriving in front of the town, they scattered the Mexicans intrenched on the outside, and then marched into the place. But the enemy had fled and gone northward to meet Fremont who was on his way from Monterey with four hundred men to attack Los Angeles.

The Mexicans had not long to search when they found

Fremont, but, instead of giving him battle, their commander surrendered, possibly preferring to give him the honor, instead of selecting the other commanders. Fremont continued his march to Los Angeles, where they went into winter quarters, and Carson, who had been devoting his valuable services to General Kearney, now rejoined his old friend, Fremont.

It may be stated in this place that the jealousy between Commodore Stockton and General Kearney assumed such a shape at that time that Fremont was compelled to acknowledge either one or the other as his superior officer. He selected Commodore Stockton as the one to whom he owed superior allegiance. The result of the petty quarrel was the trial of Fremont by court martial, the particulars of which are too well known to require further reference at our hands.

In the following March, Kit Carson was selected to carry despatches to Washington. Lieutenant Beale, who was still suffering from the exposure and hardships he had undergone, accompanied him, together with a guard of a dozen veteran mountaineers. Lieutenant Beale was so weak that Carson for many days was obliged to lift him on and off his horse; but the clear air, the healthful exercise and the cheery companionship of the hardy scout were the best tonics in the world, and probably did the invalid more good than any other treatment that could have been devised.

Carson took an extremely southern route, and his superior skill and knowledge of the country and its inhabitants enabled him to avoid all danger until he reached a tributary of the lower Colorado. While in camp at midnight, they were assailed with a shower of arrows from a party of Indians; but, as Carson expected the attack, he had made such preparations that not one of his men were injured.

Without any other incident worth the mention, Carson and his escort reached St. Louis. There the renowned mountaineer became the hero of the hour. He was taken at once to the home of Hon. Thomas H. Benton, the distinguished statesman and the father in law of Colonel Fremont, who introduced him to the leading Citizens.

The first person to greet Carson when he stepped from the cars in Washington was Mrs. Fremont, who recognized him from the description given by her husband in his letters. She compelled him to accompany her to the house of her father, where he remained an honored guest during his stay in Washington, which was for a considerable time.

Among the compliments paid Carson while in the capital was that of his appointment by President Polk, as lieutenant in the rifle corps of the United States army, and he was ordered to return across the continent with despatches. At Fort Leavenworth, Carson was furnished with an escort of fifty men who were volunteers in the war against Mexico.

The journey westward was marked by no stirring incident until he reached the eastern declivity of the Rocky Mountains, where a company of United States Volunteers were overtaken. They had in charge an enormous train of wagons on the way to New Mexico. On the morning after the encampment of Carson near them, the Indians made an attack upon the volunteers, capturing all their cattle and more than twenty horses. The mountaineer and his men dashed to the rescue, recaptured all the cattle, but were unable to retake the horses.

Shortly after, Carson and his company reached Santa Fe. There he parted from the volunteers and hired sixteen others with which he continued the journey, thereby obeying the instructions received at Fort Leavenworth.

Pursuing the even tenor of his way, he arrived at a tributary of the Virgin River, when he abruptly came upon an encampment of several hundred Comanches, who, as Carson happened to know, had massacred a number of settlers only a short time before. Understanding as thoroughly as he did the treacherous nature of these people, he made a bold front, and, when they attempted to visit his camp, peremptorily ordered them to keep away.

He added that he knew all about them, and the first one who moved closer would be shot. Furthermore, if they did not depart, within a specified time, he notified them that they would be fired upon. These were such audacious words that the Comanches doubted their sincerity. To test it, some of them overstayed their time. Not wishing to break his pledge, Carson ordered his men to fire, One of the warriors fell, while several others, who were badly wounded, came to the conclusion that when the great mountaineer made a statement there was likely to be considerable truth in it.

Food soon became so scarce that mule meat formed the only diet until they reached Los Angeles. Carson pushed on to Monterey where he delivered the despatches to the proper officer, and then returning to Los Angeles he was assigned to duty in Captain Smith's Company of United States dragoons. He was given command of twenty-five dragoons and directed to proceed to Tajon Pass, through which marauding Indians were accustomed to pass when returning from their raids in California. It was an important point, and the winter of 1847-48 was spent in the performance of the duties thus placed upon him. In the spring, he was once more ordered to carry despatches to Washington, an escort being furnished him as in the previous instance.

In crossing Grand River, one of the rafts became unmanageable, upset, losing considerable valuable property and endangering the lives of a number of the company. A large force of Utah and Apache Indians were encountered, but Carson managed them with the same skill he had shown them so many times before.

On arriving at Taos, he spent several days with his family and friends, after which he proceeded to Santa Fe. There he learned that the United States Senate had refused to confirm his nomination as lieutenant in the army. Many of his friends were so angered over this slight that they urged him to refuse to carry the despatches further; but his reply, as given by Dr. Peters, is so admirable that we quote it:

"I was entrusted with these despatches, having been chosen in California, from whence I come, as the most competent person to take them through safely. I would try to fulfill this duty even if I knew it would cost me my life. It matters not to me, while I am performing this service for my country, whether I hold the rank of lieutenant in the United States Army or am known merely as an experienced mountaineer. I have gained some little honor and credit for the manner in which I have always conducted myself when detailed on any special and important business, and I would on no account now wish to forfeit the good opinion formed of me by a majority of my countrymen because the United States Senate did not deem it proper to confer on me an appointment which I never solicited, and one which, had it been confirmed, I would have resigned at the termination of the war."

Having determined to perform his duty, he made careful inquiries as to the state of feeling among the Indians through whose country the trail led. The reports were of the most alarming character: the Comanches were on the war path with a vengeance. They were swarming all along the old Santa Fe Trail, on the watch for parties whom they could overwhelm and destroy.

Such being the case, Carson resorted to the bold artifice of making a trail of his own. He reduced his escort to ten experienced mountaineers and then struck out upon his new route. He rode northward from Taos until within a region rarely visited by hostiles, when he changed his course by the compass several times. By this means, he reached Fort Kearney on the Platte and finally arrived at Fort Leavenworth. Not only had he avoided all trouble with Indians, but by following the new route, had found abundance of game so that the entire trip was but little more than a pleasure excursion.

All danger was over at Fort Leavenworth, where he parted from his escort and went alone to Washington. Previous to this, the war with Mexico had ended, the treaty of peace having been signed February 2, 1848, and proclaimed on the 4th of July following.

Carson tarried in Washington only long enough to deliver his despatches to the proper authorities, when he turned about and made his way to Taos, New Mexico, where he joined once more his family and friends.

CHAPTER XXXI.

HOSTILITY OF THE APACHES—COLONEL BEALE SENDS AN EXPEDITION AGAINST THEM—NOTHING ACCOMPLISHED—COLONEL BEALE LEADS AN EXPEDITION WITH CARSON AS GUIDE—CAPTURE AND RELEASE OF TWO CHIEFS—MARCH TO THE ARKANSAS—ANOTHER FAILURE—CARSON AND MAXWELL BUILD A RANCHE—FREMONT'S FOURTH EXPEDITION—THE MURDEROUS APACHES—A FRUITLESS PURSUIT.

Kit Carson was one of those whose destiny seems to be that of stirring incident and adventure. No man possessed such an intimate knowledge of the manners, customs and peculiarities of the tribes in the southwest, and with his exceptional woodcraft, skill and high courage his services were always indispensable.

While he was at Taos, the Indians around him were restless until the whole country was seething and on the verge of a general revolt. Colonel Beale, commanding officer of the district, had established his headquarters at Taos. The Apaches committed so many outrages that he believed the only course open was to administer a thorough chastisement; but it was tenfold easier to reach such a conclusion than it was to carry it out. A strong force having been despatched to bring them to account, pursued them to the mountains from which they were compelled to return without accomplishing anything at all. The subsequent history of these Apaches and of General Crook's campaign against them are familiar enough to all to justify the declaration that they have proven themselves the bravest and most formidable tribe that has defied the United States government during the past half century.

Disappointed that the officer whom he sent failed to do anything, Colonel Beale took command himself and employed Kit Carson as guide. Instead of stopping in the mountains because they were blocked with snow, as the former expedition had done, Colonel Beale forced his way with great difficulty through them. The search for the Indians was long but fruitless. The cunning red skins were at home in their fastnesses and not a solitary warrior was bagged.

As the supply of provisions was running low, Colonel Beale was forced to return and retrace his steps. On their return, they came upon a village of Apaches into which the soldiers charged; but the nimble warriors easily got away, with the exception of a couple of chiefs who fell into the hands of the Americans. Hoping to rouse the chivalry and gratitude of their nature, Colonel Beale lectured them kindly and after their promise to behave themselves, allowed them to depart. As soon as they were beyond rifle shot, they must have grinned with exultation, for it was not their nature to repay kindness with anything but cruelty.

As Colonel Beale could not accomplish anything during

the winter months, he returned to Taos, where he remained until February, when, learning that a large force of Indians were congregated on the Arkansas, with a number of Mexican captives, he went thither intending to retake them by force, if they could not be secured by peaceable means. He had two companies of dragoons, and as before, engaged Carson as guide.

When he reached the Arkansas, he found himself confronted by two thousand Indians who had gathered to meet their agent and probably to consult as to their future movements. The agent was present and was a man of practical sense and experience. He told Colonel Beale that it would never do to demand the prisoners, for the Indians were in ugly temper and if aroused, would massacre the whole command. Colonel Beale himself was resentful, and very much disposed to give the red men battle, but he suffered himself to be dissuaded from carrying out his original purpose.

When Carson returned once more to Taos, he reflected that he was approaching middle life, and as he now had quite a family, he was anxious to provide something for them. Though he had rendered services beyond value to the United States government, and to different individuals, he had not received enough compensation to place them above want should he become disabled. About this time, his old friend, Maxwell, proposed that they should build a ranch in a beautiful valley some distance north of Taos. The site was a most charming one, though it was so much exposed to the attack of Indians that until then no one had dared to settle there.

Handsome, roomy and substantial structures were erected, and many of the most enjoyable days of their lives were spent on this famous ranche. It would be a pleasant farewell to leave them there to end their days in comfort and peace, but it was to be far otherwise with both and especially with Carson.

In 1848-49, Colonel Fremont made a fourth exploring expedition across the continent, he bearing all the expense, as he did in the case of his fifth expedition made in 1853. The fourth was an appalling failure, marked by an extremity of suffering that is incredible. The guide employed was wholly ignorant and the command became entangled among the snows of the mountains, where some of them lived not only on mules but on each other. The strongest lay down and died, and the horrible features of Fremont's fourth expedition were only approached by that of Lieutenant Strain on the Isthmus of Darien. When the few ghastly survivors staggered out of the mountains they tottered to Carson's ranche, where they received the kindest treatment from him who had served Fremont so faithfully on his former expeditions.

Carson had been on his ranche but a short time, when news reached him of a most atrocious murder by the Apaches. A wealthy merchant was returning in his private carriage with his wife and child from the United States to Santa Fe. He was accompanied by a small escort and the wagon train carrying his goods. When he believed all danger past, he hurried forward with his family, who were becoming tired of the journey.

At a point where there was no suspicion of danger, the Apaches fired upon the carriage, killing every one who accompanied it, including the merchant himself. The wife and child were made prisoners and carried away. Shortly after the little one was tomahawked and thrown into the river.

When news of the outrage reached New Mexico, a party

was hastily organized and started out in the hope of saving the woman and punishing the wretches who had committed the murders. When Carson learned of what was contemplated, he offered his services. They were accepted, but much to the surprise of his friends, he was given an inferior position. It was characteristic of the splendid scout that he did not show by word or look that he felt the slightest resentment on account of the slight.

With a less skilful leader than himself, Carson galloped with the company to the scene of the murder. The sight was frightfully suggestive: pieces of harness, band boxes, trunks, strips of blood stained clothing, and fragments of the carriage attested the untamable ferocity of the Apaches who had swooped down on the doomed party like a cyclone.

From that point the trail was taken and the infuriated mountaineers urged their steeds to the utmost, knowing the value of every hour and that in the case of a fight with the Indians a surprise is half the battle.

Day after day the pursuit was maintained until nearly two weeks had gone by, before the first glimpse of a warrior was obtained. The trail was one of the worst imaginable, and, had the pursuers been less skilful, they would have been baffled almost from the first. At certain points, the Apaches would break up into parties of two or three that would take different routes, reuniting at some place many miles beyond where water was known to be. This was done repeatedly, with a view of disconcerting any avengers who might take their trail, and it is a tribute to the ability of the mountaineers that the cunning artifice failed, so far as they were concerned, of its purpose.

At last the Apaches were descried in the distance. Carson was the first to discover them, he being some distance in advance. Knowing how necessary it was to surprise them he shouted to his companions to charge at once. Not doubting he would be followed, he dashed ahead with his horse on a dead run, but looking over his shoulder when he had gone part way, he saw to his consternation he was alone.

Angered and impatient, he rode back to learn what it meant. The chief guide had directed the men to wait as there was no doubt the Apaches desired to hold a parley. It meant the next moment in the shape of a bullet from the Indians which struck the leader in the breast and rendered him senseless. As soon as he recovered, he ordered his men to make the attack and leave him to himself.

He was obeyed, but the delay was fatal. On charging into the camp they were able to kill only one warrior. The body of the woman was found still warm, showing that she had been slain only a brief while before.

All those acquainted with the particulars of this sad affair agreed that had the advice of Carson been followed the poor lady might have been saved.

CHAPTER XXXII.

THE WOUNDED HERDER—A SUCCESSFUL PURSUIT—AN ATROCIOUS PLOT—HOW IT WAS FRUSTRATED—GRATITUDE OF THE GENTLEMEN WHOM CARSON WAS THE MEANS OF SAVING FROM DEATH.

Carson returned to his ranche where he spent the winter. One day in spring a wounded herder managed to reach the place with the news that he and his companion, stationed a few miles away, had been attacked by Apaches, who wounded both, and ran off all the horses and mules.

A squad of ten dragoons and a sergeant were on guard near Carson's ranche. They and three settlers, including Carson, started at once in pursuit. It was so late in the day that when they came to the place where the outrage had been committed, it was dark and they went into camp; but they were astir at the earliest dawn, and soon striking the trail of the thieves, put their animals to a keen gallop. Some twenty miles further, the Apaches were described a long distance away. As it was upon the open prairie the contest at once resolved itself into an open chase.

It was no time to spare the animals, whose rapid gait was increased until it became a killing pace. The pursuers were steadily gaining, when four of their horses succumbed and their riders, much to their chagrin, were shut out from the impending fray. The others had no time to stop: they could simply shout goodbye to them and spur their steeds to greater exertions. Fortunately the pursuers were better mounted than the fugitives who numbered a full score. With a bravery characteristic of their tribe, they clung to their stolen property, preferring to be overtaken and forced into a fight rather than abandon it.

As soon as the parties were within rifle range, the battle began and became of the most exciting character. The Apaches were splendid horsemen and displayed great skill. They threw themselves on the far side of their steeds, firing from under the neck, and keeping their bodies so well concealed that it was a difficult task to bring them down.

But the white men were accustomed to that sort of work, and the Apaches learned a lesson they never forgot. Five of their best warriors were killed, several badly wounded and nearly all the animals recaptured. Kit Carson directed every movement of his men and to that fact their great success was due.

The mountaineer was favored with prosperous times on his ranche. He and a companion drove fifty head of mules and horses to Fort Laramie, where they were disposed of at a liberal profit. The round journey of a thousand miles was attended with much danger, but it was accomplished without mishap.

He reached home just in time to learn that the Apaches had visited the little settlement and run off all the animals. But as enough soldiers were within call, a pursuit was soon organized and very nearly all the stock was recovered.

Some months later an officer of the United States Army in

Taos learned of a most atrocious plot that was on foot. Two wealthy gentlemen, travelling leisurely through that section of the country, had engaged an American named Fox to hire enough men to escort them across the plains. This Fox was one of the most conscienceless wretches and desperadoes that ever lived. He formed a scheme to murder the two gentlemen at a certain point on the plains and to divide their money among him and his companions. Those whom he secured were taken into his confidence and agreed to the crime before hand.

Among those to whom he applied was a miscreant in Taos, who, for some reason, refused to go with him. However, he kept the secret until sure the entire party were so far out on the plains that nothing could prevent the perpetration of the crime. He then told it to several associates, one of whom made it known to the officer of whom we have spoken.

This gentleman was horrified, and uncertain what could be done, if indeed he could do anything, hastened to Kit Carson, to whom he made known the story. The mountaineer listened eagerly, and, as soon as he grasped the whole plot, declared there was reason to believe it was not too late to frustrate it. With that wonderful intuition which was such a marked characteristic of his nature, he fixed upon the very place where it had been decided the crime was to be committed. Knowing the entire route, it was easy to determine the spot most likely to be selected, which was more than two hundred miles distant. Instead, therefore, of following the trail, he struck directly across the open prairie by the most direct course to his destination.

Ten finely mounted dragoons accompanied, all ready for any deed of daring. The route led through a country where the Indians were very hostile, but they were avoided with little difficulty. The second night out, they came upon the encampment of a detachment of United States troops, whose captain volunteered to take twenty of his soldiers and help bring the desperadoes to justice.

The expedition was a complete success. They overtook the party at the very spot fixed upon, and Fox was arrested before he suspected the business of the strangers in camp. When the overthrow of the wretches was complete, the gentlemen were told the story. They were speechless for a moment and could not believe it; but the proof was complete, and they turned pale at the thought of the fate they had escaped.

Their gratitude was unbounded. Taking the hand of Carson they begged him to name some reward he would accept, but the mountaineer shook his head.

"I am more than repaid in being able to help frustrate such a crime as was contemplated; I cannot think of accepting anything of the kind you name."

The gentlemen, however, could not forget that under heaven, they owed their lives to Kit Carson. The following spring a couple of splendid revolvers arrived at the mountaineer's ranche addressed to him. Beautifully engraved on them were a few sentences expressive of the feelings of the donors and the special occasion which called forth the gift.

It is easy to understand how much more acceptable such an acknowledgement was to Kit Carson than any sum of money could have been.

Fox was lodged in jail, but though there was no doubt of his guilt in the minds of every one, yet the meditated crime was so difficult to establish that ultimately he was set free.

CHAPTER XXXIII.

CARSON VISITS ST. LOUIS ON BUSINESS—ENCOUNTER WITH CHEYENNE ON HIS RETURN—HIS SAGACITY DOES NOT FAIL HIM—CARSON'S LAST BEAVER EXPEDITION—HIS CALIFORNIA SPECULATION.

Maxwell, the mountaineer and intimate friend of Carson, was quite wealthy and was of great assistance in several schemes which they undertook in partnership. One of their enterprises was that of sending a train of wagons belonging to the two to the States. Carson took charge, and, jogging along at a comfortable rate, they reached in due time the Missouri, where he went by steamboat to St. Louis. There he purchased a large amount of merchandise which was taken up stream on the boat, transferred to his wagon train, and the faces of all were then turned toward New Mexico.

Everything went well until they approached the fording of the Arkansas, when they came upon a large village of Cheyenne Indians. Unfortunately some days before, a company of recruits had shown such cruelty toward several warriors belonging to that tribe, that they were roused to the highest point of fury, and were only waiting an opportunity to visit punishment on the first whites that came in their way.

Carson knew nothing of the occurrence nor did he know of the bitter hostility of the Cheyennes, but when they went into council, and he overheard some expressions, he saw that something was wrong. He warned his men to be ready for instant attack, never permitting the Indians to catch them off their guard for a single moment.

The warriors fell behind, but after awhile, a number rode up on horseback. They were in their war paint and there could be no doubt of their hostility. Carson spoke in a conciliating manner and invited them into his camp to have a smoke and talk. The invitation was accepted. The hypocritical ceremony continued some time, when the warriors began talking among themselves.

They spoke in Sioux at first, their purpose being to lay the impending massacre against those people, but in their excitement, they dropped back to their own tongue and the whole appalling truth became speedily known to Carson and through him to his companions.

He sat on the ground with the furious warriors, and heard them agree that at the moment the leader (as they recognized Carson to be), laid down his arms to take the pipe in his mouth, they would leap upon and kill him. They would then massacre all the rest. Inasmuch as they were powerful enough to carry out this diabolical plan, it will be admitted that Carson's nerves were pretty thoroughly tested, when the pipe passing from one to the other was within a few minutes of reaching him.

Most of the men with the mountaineer were Mexicans, very deficient in courage and in a hand to hand encounter, the Cheyennes could overcome the party in the space of a few minutes.

It was in such crises as these that the remarkable fertility of resources possessed by Kit Carson displayed themselves. He seemed to perceive by intuition the wisest course to adopt and that perception came to him the instant the demand for it appeared.

Rising to his feet and grasping his weapons, he strode to the middle of the group and astounded them by beginning his address in their native tongue. He reminded them that that was proof he comprehended every word uttered by them. He spoke as if grieved by their course, for he insisted he had never wronged any one of their tribe, but on the contrary had been their friend. He then commanded them to leave the camp without delay or they would be riddled with bullets.

Carson's blue eyes flashed and his face was like a thunder cloud. It was the Cheyennes who were surprised and they could but obey orders, though from their manner, it was clear the trouble was not yet ended. They withdrew and went into council, while Carson and his friends pushed rapidly forward.

The peril in which this little command was placed could not be overestimated. There were not twenty men all told and except two or three, were Mexicans who in no respect were the superiors if indeed they were the equals of the Cheyennes. Had Carson been absent a score of warriors could have charged into camp and slain every one. Instead of a score there were several hundred of them: if they chose to make the attack he knew there was no escape.

The horses, therefore, were lashed to do their utmost. The train pushed forward with all speed, while the apprehensive leader continually glanced back over the prairie, almost certain of seeing the Cheyennes galloping toward them. When night came, there was little sleep in camp. Nearly every one stood on guard, but the night and the following day passed without molestation.

Convinced beyond question that the attack would be made unless some extraordinary means was taken to avert it, Carson took one of the fleetest footed Mexican boys outside the camp, and, pointing in the direction of the ranche of himself and Maxwell, nearly three hundred miles away, told him he must make all speed thither, and tell the soldiers that unless they hurried to his help he and all his companions were doomed to certain death at the hands of an overwhelming war party of Cheyennes. Everything depended on the quickness with which the Mexican youth brought assistance. The latter being promised a liberal reward, bounded away with the fleetness of a deer, and quickly vanished in the gloom. He went on foot because he could travel faster and last longer than could any animal in camp that he might ride.

Carson went back to his friends and kept watch until morning. As soon as it came to light, the animals were hitched to the wagons and urged forward again to the fullest extent of their ability.

Some hours later, several Cheyenne horsemen were seen riding rapidly toward them. When a hundred yards distant, Carson compelled them to halt. Then he allowed them to come closer and told them he had lost patience with their annoyances, and the night before had sent an express to Rayado (where his ranche was built), asking the troops to see that the persecution was stopped. Should it so happen that the soldiers came and found the party massacred, they would take the trail of the Cheyennes and punish them for what they had done.

The cunning Indians, before accepting the statement of the leader, said they would examine the prairie for the trail of the messenger. Carson assisted them in the search, and it did not take long to find the moccasin tracks. A brief scrutiny also satisfied the warriors he had started so many hours before, that it was useless to try to overtake him.

The result was the attack and massacre were not made, and, though the assistance which was asked was sent, yet it was not needed. One of the two experienced mountaineers with Carson on that eventful journey, declared afterward, that had any other living man than he been at the head of the party not one would have escaped. The achievement certainly ranks among the most extraordinary of the many performed by a most extraordinary man.

It would be thought that after such an experience, Carson would be content to settle down and give his entire attention to his ranche. While it cannot be said that he neglected his duties as a farmer, yet he loved the mountains and prairies too well ever to abandon them altogether.

He and Maxwell, his old friend, determined on having one more old fashioned beaver hunt, such as they were accustomed to a score of years before. They did not mean it should be child's play and they admitted no amateur hunters and trappers: all were veterans of years' standing, and, when the party was fully made up, they numbered about a score.

The expedition was a memorable one. They fixed upon one of the longest and most dangerous routes, which included many Rocky Mountain streams and involved every possible kind of danger.

In one respect, the party were pleasantly disappointed. Years before the beavers had been so effectively cleaned out that they expected to find very few if any; but because the business had been so little followed for so long a time, the animals had increased very fast and therefore the trappers met with great success.

They began operation on the South Fork of the Platte and finally ended on the Arkansas. They were gone many weeks and when they returned to their homes, nearly if not all felt that they had engaged on their last trapping expedition.

Carson had not wrought very long on his ranche, when he learned of the scarcity and high prices of sheep in California. He at once set about collecting several thousand, hired a number of men and drove the herd to Fort Laramie: thence he made his way by the old emigrant trail to California where he disposed of the sheep at prices which brought him a profit of several thousand dollars.

While in San Francisco, he visited a prominent restaurant where he ordered a good substantial dinner for six persons. When it was ready he surveyed it for a moment with satisfaction, and, seating himself at the table, disposed of it all. His journey across the plains had given him a somewhat vigorous appetite.

CHAPTER XXXIV.

IN SAN FRANCISCO—THE RETURN HOMEWARD—
THE MORMON DELEGATE GIVES CARSON SOME
INTERESTING INFORMATION—CARSON'S FIRST
STIRRING DUTIES AS INDIAN AGENT—THE
AFFECTION OF THE RED MEN FOR FATHER KIT.

Kit Carson's old friend, Maxwell, who had been his companion in so many stirring adventures, joined him in San Francisco, whose marvellous growth even at that remote day was a continual surprise and delight. As the two veteran mountaineers made their way through the streets, where but a few years before all was a wild, untrodden wilderness, they paused and indulged in many wondering exclamations as though they were a couple of countrymen visiting the metropolis for the first time in their lives.

The couple concluded to make their way home by the southern route, passing in the neighborhood of the Gila; but the distance could be shortened so much by taking the steamer to Los Angeles that Maxwell decided to adopt that course. When he asked Carson to join him the mountaineer shook his head.

"I got enough of that in 1846," he said, alluding to his brief voyage, when serving under Fremont in California, at the beginning of the Mexican war; "I never was so sick in all my life."

"You ain't likely to be sick again," plead Maxwell; "and, if you are, it don't last long. You'll save two or three weeks in time and enjoy yourself much more."

But it was no use: Carson said he never would venture upon salt water again, and he would rather ride a thousand miles on the back of a mule than to sail a hundred in a ship. Accordingly, the party separated for the time and Maxwell took steamer to Los Angeles, where he arrived fully two weeks in advance of Carson, who rode into the quaint old town on the back of a somewhat antiquated mule.

They were soon ready for their long ride, when they struck a leisurely pace and all went well until they reached the Gila. There they entered a region which had been visited by one of those droughts which continue sometimes for many months. The grass was so dry and parched that it contained scarcely any nourishment, and the friendly Pimos told them if they pushed on their animals were sure to die of starvation. It was impossible to doubt these statements and Carson therefore proposed a new route, which though very rough and difficult in some places, would furnish all the forage that was required.

The course led them along the Gila to the mouth of the San Pedro, and finally with little difficulty they reached the copper mines of New Mexico. Shortly after Carson encountered the Mormon delegate to Congress. During the exchange of courtesies, the gentleman conveyed the interesting information that he—Carson—had been made Indian Agent for New Mexico.

The news was a surprise and a great pleasure to the

mountaineer. He had no thought of any such honor and with all his modesty could not but feel that he was eminently fitted for the performance of its duties. No one had travelled so extensively through the west, and no one could understand the nature of native Americans better than he. A hundred tribes knew of "Father Kit," as he soon came to be called, and they referred to him as a man who never spoke with a "double tongue," and who was just toward them at all times. He had ventured among the hostiles more than once where the bravest white man dared not follow him, and had spent days and nights in their lodges without being offered the slightest indignity. Kit Carson was brave, truthful, kind and honest.

Aside from the gratification which one naturally feels, when receiving an appointment that is pleasant in every respect, and which he holds thoroughly "in hand," as may be said, the honest mountaineer was especially delighted over the thought that his government conferred it without any solicitation on his part.

But the man who accepts the position of Indian Agent and conscientiously attends to its duties has no sinecure on his hands. Many of them use it as such while others do still worse, thereby sowing the seeds which speedily develop into Indian outrages, massacres and wars.

When Carson reached Taos, he had his official bond made out, and sent it with his thanks and acceptance of his appointment to the proper authorities in Washington.

The Indian Agent for New Mexico had scarcely entered upon his new duties, when trouble came. A branch of the Apaches became restless and committed a number of outrages on citizens. Stern measures only would answer and a force of dragoons were sent against them. They dealt them a severe blow, killing one of their most famous chiefs, besides a considerable number of warriors.

Instead of quieting the tribe, it rather intensified their anger, though they remained quiescent for a time through fear. Not long after, Carson was notified that a large party of the tribe were encamped in the mountains, less than twenty miles from Taos. He decided at once to supplement the work of the sword with the gentle arguments of peace.

This proceeding on the part of the Indian Agent is one deserving of special notice, for it shows no less the bravery of Carson than it does the philanthropic spirit which actuated him at all times in his dealings with the red men. Alas, that so few of our officials today deem his example worth their imitation.

The venture was so dangerous that Carson went alone, unwilling that any one else should run the risk. When he arrived at their encampment, he made his way without delay to the presence of the leaders, whom he saluted in the usual elaborate fashion, and then proceeded to state the important business that took him thither.

Nearly every warrior in camp recognized the short, thickset figure and the broad, pleasant face when they presented themselves. They knew he was one of the most terrible warriors that ever charged through a camp of red men. He had met them many a time in fierce warfare, but he always fought warriors and not papooses and squaws. He was the bravest of the brave and therefore they respected him.

But he was a truthful and just man. He had never lied to them, as most of the white men did, and he had shown his confidence in them by walking alone and unattended into the very heart of their encampment. They were eager to rend to shreds every pale face upon whom they could lay hands, but "Father Kit" was safe within their lodges and wigwams.

Carson made an admirable speech. He at first caused every serpent-like eye to sparkle, by his delicate flattery. Then he tried hard to convince them that their hostility to the whites could result only in injury to themselves, since the Great Father at Washington had hundreds and thousands of warriors whom he would send to replace such as might lose their lives. Then, when he made known that the same Great Father had appointed him to see that justice was done them, they grinned with delight and gathering around, overwhelmed him with congratulations.

The Agent insisted that they should prove their sincerity by pledging to follow the line of conduct he had lain down, and they did so with such readiness that a superficial observer would have declared the mission a complete success.

But Kit Carson thought otherwise. He knew the inherent treachery of the aboriginal nature, and his estimate of Apache loyalty was the true one. The most that he was warranted in feeling was the hope that those furious warriors would be less aggressive than had been their custom. Though they had expressed a willingness to make any agreement which he might propose, yet it was their very willingness to do so which caused his distrust. Had they been more argumentative and more tenacious of their rights, their sincerity might have been credited.

The Agent could have secured their consent almost to any agreement, but the sagacious official asked as little as he could.

"And I don't believe they mean to keep even that agreement," he muttered, as he bade the effusive sachems and warriors goodbye and made his way back to Taos.

CHAPTER XXXV.

TROUBLE WITH THE APACHES—DEFEAT OF THE SOLDIERS—COLONEL COOK'S EXPEDITION AGAINST THEM—IT MEETS WITH ONLY PARTIAL SUCCESS—MAJOR BROOKS' ATTEMPT TO PUNISH THE APACHES—A THIRD EXPEDITION.

Just as Carson suspected, the Apaches were insincere in their professions of good will toward the settlers. He had scarcely reached home, when they renewed their outrages. The sinewy horsemen, as daring as the Crusaders who invaded the Holy Land, seemed to be everywhere. We have already referred to those extraordinary warriors, who, for many years have caused our Government more trouble in the southwest than all the other tribes combined, and it is not necessary, therefore, to say that when any branch of the Apaches went on the war path the most frightful scenes were sure to follow.

Carson knew when to be gentle and when to be stern. If the former measures failed, he did not hesitate to use the latter. Coercive means were taken, but, in the first encounter between the red men and the United States troops, the latter were decisively defeated.

As a consequence, the Apaches became more troublesome

than ever. Colonel Cook of the Second Regiment of United States Dragoons, was sent against them. He selected Kit Carson for his guide. The Agent's wish, it may be said, was to learn whether any other tribe was concerned in the outrages, and in no way could he do it as well as by accompanying the expedition, which was fully organized by the selection of a number of Pueblo Indians to act as scouts and spies. These were placed under the immediate command of the well known James H. Quinn, who died some time later.

The force proceeded northward from Taos to the stream known as the Arroya Hondo. This was followed to the Rio del Norte, which being very high, was crossed with much difficulty. As an illustration of the rugged work which such expeditions were called upon to undergo, Dr. Peters says that when they struggled to the other shore, they found themselves confronted by a mass of solid and almost perpendicular rocks, fully six hundred feet high. This was ascended, after the most exhausting labor, by means of a zigzag trail, and the journey was pushed over a rough and diversified country. Grass and water could not be found until they reached a small Mexican town where they were enabled to buy what was so sadly needed. Men and animals were so worn out that they rested for an entire day.

The next morning the line of march was taken up, and they had not gone far when Carson discovered a trail. This was followed with renewed vigor and a couple of days later the Indians were overtaken. They did not attempt any stand against such a strong force, but took to flight at once. The Apaches used their utmost endeavors to get away and they were helped by the roughness of the country. They were pressed so hard, however, that they lost most of their horses and plunder besides a number of warriors.

Two Americans were wounded, one of whom shortly died; but the soldiers having "located" the Indians, as may be said, did not give over their efforts to punish them. Pursuit was resumed at earliest daylight and men and animals did everything possible. Over mountains, through ravines, around rocks, up and down declivities, the chase continued, until the cunning Apaches resorted to their old tricks: they dissolved, as may be said, into their "original elements"—that is, they began separating until there were almost as many different trails as there were warriors. Then in their flight, they selected the worst possible ground. Being familiar with the country and possessing far more endurance than the ordinary Indian, it soon became clear that the marauders were beyond reach.

Accordingly Colonel Cook ordered the pursuit discontinued and they headed toward the nearest Mexican village, where forage and rest could be secured for the animals. When the place was reached, Colonel Cook learned of a serious mistake made by the party who were transporting the soldier wounded several days before. They discovered an Indian whom, after some difficulty, they captured. His horse and arms were taken from him under the supposition that he was one of the hostile Apaches. He was not treated very gently and watching his opportunity, he made his escape. It was afterwards learned that the warrior was a Utah, with whom the white men were at peace.

The Utahs were of a war-like nature and Colonel Cook was apprehensive they would use the occurrence as a pretext for joining the Apaches in their attack upon the settlers. He therefore sent Carson to the headquarters of his agency to do what he could to explain the matter and make all the reparation in his power.

As soon as he arrived at Taos, Carson sent a messenger with a request that the Utah chiefs would come and have a talk with him. They were always glad to meet Father Kit face to face. The agent told how the mistake was made, expressed the regret of himself and Colonel Cook and ended by restoring the property and by distributing a few presents among the chiefs. The business was managed with such tact that the sachems expressed themselves perfectly satisfied and their affection and admiration for Father Kit became greater than before.

Colonel Cook was unwilling to return without striking a more effective blow against the Apaches. Pausing only long enough, therefore, to rest and recruit his men and horses, he resumed the hunt. He had not gone far, when he struck another trail which was followed with great vigor; but before anything of the Indians could be discovered, it began snowing. In a few minutes the flakes were eddying all around them, the wind blowing so furiously that the men could hardly see each other, as they bent their heads and rode slowly against it. This rendered pursuit out of the question, because the trail was entirely hidden. Much against his will Colonel Cook was forced to give up the pursuit.

He made his way to a small town lying on his route, where he met Major Brooks, who was marching to his help with reinforcements. The latter officer instead of returning with Colonel Cook, decided to take up the hunt himself for the hostiles.

With little delay, a fresh trail was found and an energetic pursuit began. It was plain the Indians were making for the Utah country, and they were pursued without difficulty; but, when that section was reached, the soldiers came upon so many trails, which crossed and recrossed so many times that all individuality was lost. The most skilful scouts in the company were unable to identify or follow any one with certainty.

The situation was exasperating, but there was no help for it and the command was compelled to turn about and make their way home, having been in the field more than two weeks without accomplishing anything at all.

But it was known that the Apaches would speedily reorganize and the soldiers had but to wait a short while, when an opportunity would be presented for striking an effective blow. When a sufficient period had elapsed, another expedition was sent out under the command of Major Carleton, of the First Regiment of United States Dragoons. He engaged Kit Carson to act as his guide.

The force marched northward about a hundred miles to Fort Massachusetts, where all the arrangements were completed. The party was divided, the spies under Captain Quinn being sent to examine the country on the west side of the White Mountains, while the Major decided to inspect the territory to the eastward of the range.

Captain Quinn with his skilful trailers moved up the San Luis Valley until he reached the famous Mosco Pass, which was often used by the Apaches when hard pressed. They were perfectly familiar with all its diverse and peculiar windings, and, when they once dashed in among the rocks, they felt safe against any and all pursuers.

Making their way through this pass, Captain Quinn and his scouts reached Wet Mountain Valley, where he had promised to meet and report to his superior officer.

CHAPTER XXXVI.

DISCOVERY OF THE TRAIL—PRAIRIE DETECTIVES.

Meanwhile, Kit Carson, who was with Major Carleton, had discovered a trail made by three of the enemy. Carefully following it up, it was found to join the principal path, a short distance away. When Quinn arrived he had also some discoveries to report, and the scouts held a consultation over the question. It was agreed by all that they were on the track of the enemy they were seeking.

The general reader is not apt to appreciate the skill, patience and intelligence shown by the scouts and hunters in tracing the flight of an enemy through a wild and desolate country. As an evidence of the wonderful attainments of border men in woodcraft, the following letter may be given, written by the surgeon at Fort Randall in Dacotah in 1869:

"The most extraordinary skill that is exhibited in this part of the country, either by the white man, or red native, is in the practice of trailing. Here it may be accounted an art as much as music, painting or sculpture is in the East. The Indian or trapper that is a shrewd trailer, is a man of close observation, quick perception, and prompt action. As he goes along, nothing escapes his observation, and what he sees and hears he accounts for immediately. Often not another step is taken until a mystery that may present itself in this line is fairly solved. The Indian trailer will stand still for hours in succession, to account for certain traces or effects in tracks, and sometimes gives to the matter unremitting attention for days and weeks.

"The trailer is not a graceful man. He carries his head much inclined, his eye is quick and restless, always on the watch, and he is practising his art unconsciously, hardly ever crossing the track of man or animal without seeing it. When he enters a house, he brings the habits he contracted in the practice of his art with him. I know a trailer as soon he enters my room. He comes in through the door softly, and with an air of exceeding caution. Before he is fairly in, or at least has sat down, he has taken note of every article and person. Though there may be a dozen vacant chairs in the room, he is not used to chairs, and, like the Indian, prefers a more humble seat. When I was employed by General Harney last summer to take charge temporarily of the Indians that were gathered here to form a new reservation, one day a guide and trailer came into the General's headquarters. I told him to be seated. He sat down on the floor, bracing his back against the wall. The General saw this, and in vexation cried out, 'My God, why don't you take a chair when there are plenty here not occupied?' The man arose and seated himself in a chair, but in so awkward and uncomfortable a manner that he looked as if he might slip from it at any moment. But when this uncouth person came to transact his business with the General, he turned out to be a man of no ordinary abilities. His description of a route he took as guide and trailer for the Ogallalas in bringing them from the Platte to this place was minute, and to me exceedingly interesting. Every war party that for the season had crossed his trail, he described with minuteness as to their number, the kinds of arms they had, and stated the tribes they belonged to. In these strange revelations that he made there was neither imposition nor supposition, for he gave satisfactory reasons for every assertion he made.

"I have rode several hundred miles with an experienced guide and trailer, Hack, whom I interrogated upon many points in the practice of this art. Nearly all tracks I saw, either old or new, as a novice in the art, I questioned him about. In going to the Niobrara River crossed the track of an Indian pony. My guide followed the track a few miles and then said, 'It is a stray, black horse, with a long, bushy tail, nearly starved to death, has a split hoof of the left fore foot, and goes very lame, and he passed here early this morning.' Astonished and incredulous, I asked him the reasons for knowing these particulars by the tracks of the animal, when he replied:

"'It was a stray horse, because it did not go in a direct line; his tail was long, for he dragged it over the snow; in brushing against a bush he left some of his hair which shows its color. He was very hungry, for, in going along, he has nipped at those high, dry weeds, which horses seldom eat. The fissure of the left fore foot left also its track, and the depth of the indentation shows the degree of his lameness; and his tracks show he was here this morning, when the snow was hard with frost.'

"At another place we came across an Indian track, and he said, 'It is an old Yankton who came across the Missouri last evening to look at his traps. In coming over he carried in his right hand a trap, and in his left a lasso to catch a pony which he had lost. He returned without finding the horse, but had caught in the trap he had out a prairie wolf, which he carried home on his back and a bundle of kinikinic wood in his right hand.' Then, he gave his reasons: 'I know he is old, by the impression his gait has made and a Yankton by that of his moccasin. He is from the other side of the river, as there are no Yanktons on this side. The trap he carried struck the snow now and then, and in same manner as when he came, shows that he did not find his pony. A drop of blood in the centre of his tracks shows that he carried the wolf on his back, and the bundle of kinikinic wood he used for a staff for support, and catching a wolf, shows that he had traps out.' But I asked, 'how do you know it is wolf; why not a fox, or a coyote, or even a deer?' Said he: 'If it had been a fox, or coyote or any other small game he would have slipped the head of the animal in his waist belt, and so carried it by his side, and not on his shoulders. Deer are not caught by traps but if it had been a deer, he would not have crossed this high hill, but would have gone back by way of the ravine, and the load would have made his steps still more tottering.'

"Another Indian track which we saw twenty miles west of this he put this serious construction upon: 'He is an upper Indian—a prowling horse thief—carried a double shot gun, and is a rascal that killed some white man lately, and passed here one week ago; for,' said he, 'a lone Indian in these parts is on mischief, and generally on the lookout for horses. He had on the shoes of a white man whom he had in all probability killed, but his steps are those of an Indian. Going through the ravine, the end of his gun hit into the deep snow. A week ago we had a very warm day, and the snow being soft, he made these deep tracks; ever since it has been intensely cold weather, which makes very shallow tracks.' I suggested that perhaps he bought those shoes. 'Indians don't buy shoes, and if they did they would not buy them as large as these were, for Indians have very small feet.'

"The most noted trailer of this country was Paul Daloria, a half breed, who died under my hands of Indian consumption last summer. I have spoken of him in a former letter. At one time I rode with him, and trailing was naturally the subject of our conversation. I begged to trail with him an old track over the prairie, in order to learn its history. I had hardly made the proposition, when he drew up his horse, which was at a ravine, and said, 'Well, here is an old elk track. Let us get off our horses and follow it.' We followed it but a few rods, when he said, it was exactly a month old, and made at 2 o'clock in the afternoon. This he knew, as then we had our last rain, and at the hour named the ground was softer than at any other time. The track before us was then made. He broke up here and there clusters of grass that lay in the path of the track, and showed me the dry ends of some, the stumps of others, and by numerous other similar items accounted for many circumstances that astonished me. We followed the trail over a mile. Now and then we saw that a wolf, a fox, and other animals had practised their trailing instincts on the elk's tracks. Here and there, he would show me where a snake, a rat, and a prairie dog had crossed the track. Nothing had followed or crossed the track that the quick eye of Daloria did not detect. He gave an account of the habits of all the animals that had left their footprints on the track, also of the state of the weather since the elk passed, and the effect of sunshine, winds, aridity, sand storms, and other influences that had a bearing on these tracks."

CHAPTER XXXVII.

THE PURSUIT AND ATTACK—TWO O'CLOCK.

When Kit Carson and the other scouts found the main trail, they eagerly took up the pursuit. They had not gone far when all doubt was removed: they were upon the track of a large hostile body of warriors and were gaining steadily; but so rapid was the flight of the marauders that it was not until the sixth day that the first glimpse of the Indians was obtained. They were encamped on a mountain peak, devoid of trees, and seemingly beyond the reach of danger; but such was the energy of the attack that they reached camp before the Indians could collect their animals and make off. The fight was a hot one for a few minutes during which quite a number of warriors were killed and wounded.

When night came a squad of men hid themselves near the camp, from which the Indians had fled, in the expectation that some of them would steal back during the darkness to learn what had been done. The dismal hours passed until near midnight, when one of the soldiers made the call which the Apaches use to hail each other. The sound had hardly died out, when two squaws and two warriors appeared and began groping silently around in the gloom. The soldiers were cruel enough to fire upon the party, but in the darkness only one was killed.

Dr. Peters states that on the morning of the day when the Apache encampment was discovered Kit Carson, after diligently studying the trail, rode up to Major Carleton and told him that if no accident intervened, the Indians would be overtaken at two o'clock in the afternoon. The officer smiled and said if the Agent proved a genuine prophet, he would present him with the finest hat that could be bought in the United States.

The pursuit continued for hours, and, when the watches in the company showed that it was two o'clock, Carson triumphantly pointed to the mountain peak, far in advance where the Indian encampment was in plain sight. He had hit the truth with mathematical exactness.

Major Carleton kept his promise. To procure such a hat as he felt he had earned, required several months; but one day the Indian Agent at Taos received a superb piece of head gear within which was the following inscription:

AT 2 O'CLOCK. KIT CARSON, FROM MAJOR CARLETON.

Dr. Peters adds that a gentleman who was a member of the expedition subjected Carson some years later to a similar test, and he came within five minutes of naming the precise time when a band of fugitives was overtaken.

Having done all that was possible, Major Carleton returned with his command to Taos and Carson resumed his duties as Indian Agent. Some months later, another expedition was organized against the Apaches but it accomplished nothing. In the latter part of the summer Carson started on a visit to the Utahs. They were under his especial charge and he held interviews with them several times a year, they generally visiting him at his ranche, which they were glad to do, as they were sure of being very hospitably treated.

This journey required a horseback ride of two or three hundred miles, a great portion of which was through the Apache country. These Indians were in such a resentful mood towards the whites that they would have been only too glad to wrench the scalp of Father Kit from his crown; but he knew better than to run into any of their traps. He was continually on the lookout, and more than once detected their wandering bands in time to give them the slip. He was equally vigilant and consequently equally fortunate on his return.

Carson found when he met the Indians in council that they had good cause for discontent. One of their leading warriors had been waylaid and murdered by a small party of Mexicans. The officials who were with Carson promised that the murderers should be given up. It was the intention of all that justice should be done, but, as was too often the case, it miscarried altogether. Only one of the murderers was caught and he managed to escape and was never apprehended again.

To make matters worse, some of the blankets which the Superintendent had presented the Indians a short while before, proved to be infected with small pox and the dreadful disease carried off many of the leading warriors of the tribe. More than one Apache was resolute in declaring the proceeding premeditated on the part of the whites. The result was the breaking out of a most formidable Indian war. The Muache band of Utahs, under their most distinguished chieftain, joined the Apaches in waylaying and murdering travellers, attacking settlements and making off with the prisoners, besides capturing hundreds and thousands of cattle, sheep, mules and horses. For a time they overran a large portion of the territory of New Mexico. Matters at last reached such a pass, that unless the savages were checked, they would annihilate all the whites.

The Governor issued a call for volunteers. The response was prompt, and five hundred men were speedily equipped and put into the field. They were placed under charge of Colonel T. T. Fauntleroy, of the First Regiment of United States Dragoons. He engaged Kit Carson as his chief guide.

The campaign was pushed with all possible vigor, but for a time nothing important was done. The weather became intensely cold. On the second campaign, Colonel Fauntleroy surprised the main camp of the enemy and inflicted great slaughter. A severe blow was administered, but the reader knows that the peace which followed proved only temporary. The Apaches have been a thorn in our side for many years. General Crook has shown great tact, bravery and rare skill in his dealings with them and probably has brought about the most genuine peace that has been known for a generation.

It would not be worth while to follow Kit Carson on his round of duties as Indian Agent. He had to deal with the most turbulent tribes on the continent, and enough has been told to prove his peerless sagacity in solving the most difficult questions brought before him. He rode thousands of miles, visiting remote points, conferred with the leading hostiles, risked his life times without number, and was often absent from home for weeks and months. While it was beyond the attainment of human endeavor for him to make an end of wars on the frontiers, yet he averted many and did a degree of good which is beyond all calculation.

"I was in the insignificant settlement of Denver, in the

autumn of 1860," said A. L. Worthington, "when a party of Arapahoes, Cheyennes and Comanches returned from an expedition against the tribe of mountain Indians know as the Utes. The allied forces were most beautifully whipped and were compelled to leave the mountains in the greatest hurry for their lives. They brought into Denver one squaw and her half dozen children as prisoners. The little barbarians, when the other youngsters came too near or molested them, would fight like young wild cats. The intention of the captors, as I learned, was to torture the squaw and her children to death. Before the arrangements were completed, Kit Carson rode to the spot and dismounted. He had a brief, earnest talk with the warriors. He did not mean to permit the cruel death that was contemplated, but instead of demanding the surrender of the captives, he ransomed them all, paying ten dollars a piece. After they were given up, he made sure that they were returned to their tribe in the mountains."

This anecdote may serve as an illustration of scores of similar duties in which the agent was engaged. It was during the same year that Carson received an injury which was the cause of his death. He was descending a mountain, so steep that he led his horse by a lariat, intending, if the animal fell, to let go of it in time to prevent being injured. The steed did fall and though Carson threw the lariat from him, he was caught by it, dragged some distance and severely injured.

When the late Civil War broke out and most of our troops were withdrawn from the mountains and plains, Carson applied to President Lincoln for permission to raise a regiment of volunteers in New Mexico, for the purpose of protecting our settlements there. Permission was given, the regiment raised and the famous mountaineer did good service with his soldiers. On one occasion he took 9,000 Navajo prisoners with less than 600 men.

At the close of the war, he was ordered to Fort Garland, where he assumed command of a large region. He was Brevet Brigadier General and retained command of a battalion of New Mexico volunteers.

Carson did not suffer immediately from his injury, but he found in time that a grave internal disturbance had been caused by his fall. In the spring of 1868, he accompanied a party of Ute Indians to Washington. He was then failing fast and consulted a number of leading physicians and surgeons. His disease was aneurism of the aorta which progressed fast. When his end was nigh, his wife suddenly died, leaving seven children, the youngest only a few weeks old. His affliction had a very depressing effect on Carson, who expired May 23, 1868.

CHAPTER XXXVIII.

LETTER FROM GENERAL W. T. SHERMAN, AND FROM GENERAL J. F. RUSLING.

In closing the life of Kit Carson, it will be appropriate to add two letters, which were furnished at our request:

912 GARRISON AVENUE, ST. LOUIS, MO., JUNE 25, 1884.

"Kit Carson first came into public notice by Fremont's Reports of the Exploration of the Great West about 1842-3. You will find mention of Kit Carson in my memoirs, vol. I, p. 46, 47, as bringing to us the first overland mail to California in his saddle bags. I saw but little of him afterwards till after the Civil War, when, in 1866, I was the Lieutenant General commanding the Military Division of the Missouri, with headquarters in St. Louis, and made a tour of my command, including what are now Wyoming, Colorado and New Mexico. Reaching Fort Garland, New Mexico, in September of October, 1866, I found it garrisoned by some companies of New Mexico Volunteers, of which Carson was Colonel or commanding officer. I stayed with him some days, during which we had a sort of council with the Ute Indians, of which the chief Ouray was the principal feature, and over whom Carson exercised a powerful influence.

"Carson then had his family with him—wife and half a

dozen children, boys and girls as wild and untrained as a brood of Mexican mustangs. One day these children ran through the room in which we were seated, half clad and boisterous, and I inquired, 'Kit, what are you doing about your children?'

"He replied: 'That is a source of great anxiety; I myself had no education,' (he could not even write, his wife always signing his name to his official reports). 'I value education as much as any man, but I have never had the advantage of schools, and now that I am getting old and infirm, I fear I have not done right by my children.'

"I explained to him that the Catholic College, at South Bend, Indiana, had, for some reason, given me a scholarship for twenty years, and that I would divide with him—that is let him send two of his boys for five years each. He seemed very grateful and said he would think of it.

"My recollection is that his regiment was mustered out of service that winter, 1866-7, and that the following summer, 1867, he (Carson) went to Washington on some business for the Utes, and on his return toward New Mexico, he stopped at Fort Lyon, on the upper Arkansas, where he died. His wife died soon after at Taos, New Mexico, and the children fell to the care of a brother in law, Mr. Boggs, who had a large ranche on the Purgation near Fort Lyon. It was reported of Carson, when notified that death was impending, that he said, 'Send William, (his eldest son) to General Sherman who has promised to educate him.' Accordingly, some time about the spring of 1868, there came to my house, in St. Louis, a stout boy with a revolver, Life of Kit Carson by Dr. Peters, United States Army, about $40 in money, and a letter from Boggs, saying that in compliance with the request of Kit Carson, on his death bed, he had sent William Carson to me. Allowing him a few days of vacation with my own children, I sent him to the college at South Bend, Ind., with a letter of explanation, and making myself responsible for his expenses. He was regularly entered in one of the classes, and reported to me regularly. I found the 'Scholarship' amounted to what is known as 'tuition,' but for three years I paid all his expenses of board, clothing, books, &c., amounting to about $300 a year. At the end of that time, the Priest reported to me that Carson was a good natured boy, willing enough, but that he had no taste or appetite for learning. His letters to me confirmed this conclusion, as he could not possibly spell. After reflection, I concluded to send him to Fort Leavenworth, Kansas, to the care of General Langdon C. Easton, United States Quartermaster, with instructions to employ him in some capacity in which he could earn his board and clothing, and to get some officer of the garrison to teach him just what was necessary for a Lieutenant of Cavalry. Lieutenant Beard, adjutant of the Fifth Infantry did this. He (William Carson) was employed, as a 'Messenger,' and, as he approached his twenty-first year, under the tuition of Lieutenant Beard, he made good progress. Meantime I was promoted to General in Chief at Washington, and about 1870, when Carson had become twenty-one years of age, I applied in person to the President, General Grant, to give the son of Kit Carson, the appointment of Second Lieutenant Ninth United States Cavalry, telling him somewhat of the foregoing details. General Grant promptly ordered the appointment to issue, subject to the examination as to educational qualifications, required by the law. The usual board of officers was appointed at Fort Leavenworth and Carson was ordered before it. After careful examination, the board found him deficient in reading, writing and arithmetic. Of course he could not be commissioned. I had given him four years of my guardianship, about $1,000 of my own money, and the benefit of my influence, all in vain. By nature, he was not adapted to 'modern uses.' I accordingly wrote him that I had exhausted my ability to provide for him, and advised him to return to his uncle Boggs on the Purgation to assist him in his cattle and sheep ranche.

"I heard from him by letter once or twice afterward, in one of which he asked me to procure for him the agency for the Utes. On inquiry at the proper office in Washington, I found that another person had secured the place of which I notified him, and though of late years I have often been on the Purgation, and in the Ute country, I could learn nothing of the other children of Kit Carson, or of William, who for four years was a sort of ward to me.

"Since the building of railroads in that region, the whole character of its population is changed, and were Kit Carson to arise from his grave, he could not find a buffalo, elk or deer, where he used to see millions. He could not even recognize the country with which he used to be so familiar, or find his own children, whom he loved, and for whose welfare he felt so solicitous in his later days.

"Kit Carson was a good type of a class of men most useful in their day, but now as antiquated as Jason of the Golden Fleece, Ulysses of Troy, the Chevalier La Salle of the Lakes, Daniel Boone of Kentucky, Irvin Bridger and Jim Beckwith of the Rockies, all belonging to the dead past.

"Yours Truly,
"W. T. SHERMAN."

"TRENTON, N. J., June 23, 1884.

"In accordance with your request to give my recollections of Kit Carson, I would say that I met and spent several days with him in September, 1866, at and near Fort Garland, Colorado, on the headwaters of the Rio Grande. I was then Brevet Brigadier General and Inspector United States Volunteers, on a tour of inspection of the military depots and posts in that region and across to the Pacific. General Sherman happened there at the same time, on like duty as to his Military Division, and our joint talks, as a rule, extended far into the night and over many subjects. 'Kit' was then Brevet Brigadier General United States Volunteers, and in command of Fort Garland, and a wide region thereabouts—mostly Indian—which he knew thoroughly. Fort Garland was a typical frontier post, composed of log huts chinked with mud, rough but comfortable, and in one of these Kit then lived with his Mexican wife and several half breed children.

"He was then a man apparently about fifty years of age. From what I had read about him, I had expected to see a small, wiry man, weather-beaten and reticent; but found him to be a medium sized, rather stoutish, and quite talkative person instead. His hair was already well-silvered, but his face full and florid. You would scarcely regard him, at first sight, as a very noticeable man, except as having a well knit frame and full, deep chest. But on observing him more closely, you were struck with the breadth and openness of his brow, bespeaking more than ordinary intelligence and courage; with his quick, blue eye, that caught everything at a glance apparently—an eye beaming with kindliness and benevolence, but that could blaze with anger when aroused; and with his full, square jaw and chin, that evidently could shut as tight as Sherman's or Grant's when necessary. With nothing of the swashbuckler or Buffalo Bill—of the border ruffian or the cowboy—about him, his manners were as gentle, and his voice as soft and sympathetic, as a woman's. What impressed one most about his face was its rare kindliness and charity—that here, at last, was a natural gentleman, simple as a child but brave as a lion. He soon took our hearts by storm, and the more we saw of him the more we became impressed with his true manliness and worth. Like everybody else on the border, he smoked freely, and at one time drank considerably; but he had quit drinking years before, and said he owed his excellent health and preeminence, if he had any, to his habits of almost total abstinence. In conversation he was slow and hesitating at first, approaching almost to bashfulness, often seemingly at a loss for words; but, as he warmed up, this disappeared, and you soon found him talking glibly, and with his hands and fingers as well—rapidly gesticulating—Indian fashion. He was very conscientious, and in all our talks would frequently say: 'Now, stop gentlemen! Is this right?' 'Ought we to do this?' 'Can we do that?' 'Is this like human nature?' or words to this effect, as if it was the habit of his mind to test everything by the moral law. I think that was the predominating feature of his character—his perfect honesty and truthfulness—quite as much as his matchless coolness and courage. Said Sherman to me one day while there: 'His integrity is simply perfect. The red skins know it, and would trust Kit any day before they would us, or the President, either!' And Kit well returned their confidence, by being their steadfast, unswerving friend and ready champion.

"He talked freely of his past life, unconscious of its

Hunter Trapper, Guide, Indian Agent and Colonel U.S.A

extraordinary character. Born in Kentucky, he said, he early took to the plains and mountains, and joined the hunters and trappers, when he was so young he could not set a trap. When he became older, he turned trapper himself, and trapped all over our territories for beaver, otter, etc., from the Missouri to the Pacific, and from British America to Mexico. Next he passed into Government employ, as an Indian scout and guide, and as such piloted Fremont and others all over the Plains and through the Rocky and Sierra Nevada Mountains. Fremont, in his reports, surrounded Kit's name with a romantic valor, but he seems to have deserved it all, and more. His good sense, his large experience, and unfaltering courage, were invaluable to Fremont, and it is said about the only time the Pathfinder went seriously astray among the Mountains was when he disregarded his (Kit's) advice, and endeavored to force a passage through the Rockies northwest of Fort Garland. Kit told him the mountains could not be crossed at that time of the year; and, when Fremont nevertheless insisted on proceeding, he resigned as guide. The Pathfinder, however, went stubbornly forward, but got caught in terrible snowstorms, and presently returned—half of his men and animals having perished outright from cold and hunger. Next Kit became United States Indian Agent, and made one of the best we ever had. Familiar with the language and customs of the Indians, he frequently spent months together among them without seeing a white man, and indeed became a sort of half Indian himself. In talking with us, I noticed he frequently hesitated for the right English word; but when speaking bastard Spanish (Mexican) or Indian, with the Ute Indians there, he was as fluent as a native. Both Mexican and Indian, however, are largely pantomime, abounding in perpetual grimace and gesture, which may have helped him along somewhat. Next, when the rebellion broke out, he became a Union soldier, though the border was largely Confederate. He tendered his services to Mr. Lincoln, who at once commissioned him Colonel, and told him to take care of the frontier, as the regulars there had to come East to fight Jeff Davis. Kit straightway proceeded to raise the First Regiment of New Mexico Volunteers, in which he had little difficulty, as the New Mexicans knew him well, and had the utmost confidence in him. With these, during the war, he was busy fighting hostile Indians, and keeping others friendly, and in his famous campaign against the Navajos, in New Mexico, with only six hundred frontier volunteers captured some nine thousand prisoners. The Indians withdrew into a wild canyon, where no white man, it was said, had ever penetrated, and believed to be impregnable. But Kit pursued them from either end, and attacked them with pure Indian strategy and tactics; and the Navajos finding themselves thus surrounded, and their supplies cut off, outwitted by a keener fighter than themselves, surrendered at discretion. Then he did not slaughter them, but marched them to a goodly reservation, and put them to work herding and planting, and they had continued peaceable ever since.

"Kit seemed thoroughly familiar with Indian life and character, and it must be conceded, that no American of his time knew our aborigines better—if any so well. It must be set down to their credit, that he was their stout friend—no Boston philanthropist more so. He did not hesitate to say, that all our Indian troubles were caused originally by bad white men, if the truth were known, and was terribly severe on the brutalities and barbarities of the border. He said the Indians were very different from what they used to be, and were yearly becoming more so from contact with border ruffians and cowboys. He said he had lived for years among them with only occasional visits to the settlements, and he had never known an Indian to injure a Pale Face, where he did not deserve it; on the other hand, he had seen an Indian kill his brother even for insulting a white man in the old times. He insisted that Indians never commit outrages unless they are first provoked to them by the borderers, and that many of the peculiar and special atrocities with which they are charged are only their imitation of the bad acts of wicked white men. He pleaded for the Indians, as 'pore ignorant critters, who had no learnin', and didn't know no better,' whom we were daily robbing of their hunting grounds and homes, and solemnly asked: 'What der yer 'spose our Heavenly Father, who made both them and us, thinks of these things?' He was particularly severe upon Col. Chivington and the Sand Creek massacre of 1864, which was still fresh in the public mind, said he; 'jist to think of that dog Chivington, and his dirty hounds, up thar at Sand Creek! Whoever heerd of sich doings 'mong Christians!'

"'The pore Indians had the Stars and Stripes flying over them, our old flag thar, and they'd bin told down to Denver, that so long as they kept that flying they'd be safe enough. Well, then, one day along comes that durned Chivington and his cusses. They'd bin out several day's huntin' Hostiles, and couldn't find none nowhar, and if they had, they'd have skedaddled from 'em, you bet! So they jist lit upon these Friendlies, and massacreed 'em—yes, sir, literally massacreed 'em—in cold blood, in spite of our flag thar—yes, women and little children, even! Why, Senator Foster told me with his own lips (and him and his Committee come out yer from Washington, you know, and investigated this muss), that that thar durned miscreant and his men shot down squaws, and blew the brains out of little innocent children—pistoled little papooses in the arms of their dead mothers, and even worse than this!—them durned devils! and you call sich soldiers Christians, do ye? and pore Indians savages!'

"'I tell you what, friends; I don't like a hostile Red Skin any more than you do. And when they are hostile, I've fit 'em—fout 'em—and expect to fight 'em—hard as any man. That's my business. But I never yit drew a bead on a squaw or papoose, and I despise the man who would. 'Taint nateral for men to kill women and pore little children, and none but a coward or a dog would do it. Of course when we white men do sich awful things, why these pore ignorant critters don't know no better than to foller suit. Pore things! Pore things! I've seen as much of 'em as any man livin', and I can't help but pity 'em, right or wrong! They once owned all this country, yes, Plains and Mountains, buffalo and everything, but now they own next door to nuthin, and will soon be gone.'

"Alas, poor Kit! He has already 'gone to the Happy Hunting Grounds.' But the Indians had no truer friend, and Kit Carson would wish no prouder epitaph than this. In talking thus he would frequently get his grammar wrong, and his language was only the patois of the Border; but there was an eloquence in his eye, and a pathos in his voice, that would have touched a heart of stone, and a genuine manliness about him at all times, that would have won him hosts of friends anywhere. And so, Kit Carson, good friend, brave heart, generous soul, hail and farewell!

"Hoping these rough recollections may serve your purpose, I remain

"Very respectfully,

"Your obedient servant,

"JAMES F. RUSLING."

The following tribute to the matchless scout, hunter and guide is from the Salt Lake Tribune:

He wrote his own biography and left it where the edition will never grow dim. The alphabet he used was made of the rivers, the plains, the forests, and the eternal heights. He started in his youth with his face to the West; started toward where no trails had been blazed, where there was naught to meet him but the wilderness, the wild beast, and the still more savage man. He made his lonely camps by the rivers, and now it is a fiction with those who sleep on the same grounds that the waters in their flow murmur the great pathfinder's name. He followed the water courses to their sources, and guided by them, learned where the mountains bent their crests to make possible highways for the feet of men. He climbed the mountains and "disputed with the eagles of the crags" for points of observation; he met the wild beast and subdued him; he met the savage of the plains and of the hills, and, in his own person, gave him notice of his sovereignty in skill, in cunning and in courage. To the red man he was the voice of fate. In him they saw a materialized foreboding of their destiny. To them he was a voice crying the coming of a race against which they could not prevail; before which they were to be swept away.

www.ingramcontent.com/pod-product-compliance
Lightning Source LLC
Chambersburg PA
CBHW020229170426
43201CB00007B/362